Prepare for the Great Tribulation and the Era of Peace

Prepare for the Great Tribulation and the Era of Peace

Volume IV:
July 11, 1996 – September 30, 1996

by John Leary

Queenship
PUBLISHING COMPANY
P.O Box 42028 Santa Barbara, CA 93140-2028
(800) 647-9882 • (805) 957-4893 • Fax: (805) 957-1631

The publisher recognizes and accepts that the final authority regarding these apparitions and messages rests with the Holy See of Rome, to whose judgement we willingly submit.

– The Publisher

Cover art by Josyp Terelya

©1996 Queenship Publishing

Library of Congress Number # 96-68181

Published by:
Queenship Publishing
P.O. Box 42028
Santa Barbara, CA 93140-2028
(800) 647-9882 • (805) 957-4893 • Fax: (805) 957-1631

Printed in the United States of America

ISBN: 1-882972-91-0

Acknowledgments

It is in a spirit of deep gratitude that I would like to acknowledge first the Holy Trinity: Father, Jesus, and the Holy Spirit, the Blessed Virgin Mary and the many saints and angels who have made this book possible.

My wife, Carol, has been an invaluable partner. Her complete support of faith and prayers has allowed us to work as a team. This was especially true in the many hours of indexing and proofing of the manuscript. All of our family has been a source of care and support.

I am greatly indebted to Josyp Terelya for his very gracious offer to provide the art work for this publication. He has spent three months of work and prayer to provide us with a selection of many original pictures. He wanted very much to enhance the visions and messages with these beautiful and provocative works. You will experience some of them throughout these volumes.

A very special thank you goes to my spiritual director, Fr. Leo J. Klem, C.S.B. No matter what hour I called him, he was always there with his confident wisdom, guidance and discernment. His love, humility, deep faith and trust are a true inspiration.

My appreciation also goes to Father John V. Rosse, my good pastor at Holy Name of Jesus Church. He has been open, loving and supportive from the very beginning.

There are many friends and relatives whose interest, love and prayerful support have been a real gift from God. Our own Wednesday, Monday and First Saturday prayer groups deserve a special thank you for their loyalty and faithfulness.

Finally, I would like to thank Bob and Claire Schaefer of Queenship Publishing and their spiritual director, Fr. Luke Zimmer for providing the opportunity to bring this message of preparation, love and warnings to you the people of God.

John Leary, Jr.
January 1996

Dedication

To the Most Holy Trinity

God

The Father, Son and Holy Spirit

The Source of

All

Life, Love and Wisdom

Publisher's Foreword

John has, with some exceptions, been having visions twice a day since they began in July, 1993. The first vision of the day usually takes place during morning Mass, immediately after he receives the Eucharist. If the name of the church is not mentioned, it is a local Rochester, NY, church. When out of town, the church name is included in the text. The second vision occurs in the evening, either at Perpetual Adoration or at the prayer group that is held at John's.

Various names appear in the text. Most of the time, the names appear only once or twice. Their identity is not important to the message and their reason for being in the text is evident. First names have been used, when requested by the individual. The name Maria E., which occurs quite often, is the visionary Maria Esperanza Bianchini of Betania, Venezuela.

We are grateful to Josep Terelya for the cover art, as well as for the art throughout the book. Josyp is a well-known visionary and also, the author of *Witness* and most recently *In the Kingdom of the Spirit.*

This volume covers visions from July 11, 1996 through September 30, 1996. The volumes will now be coming out quarterly due to the urgency of the messages. Volume I contains visions from July, 1993 through June, 1994. Volume II contains visions from July, 1994 through June, 1995. Volume III contains visions from July, 1995 through July 10, 1996.

The Publisher
October, 1996

Foreword

It was in July of 1993 that Almighty God, especially through Jesus, His Eternal Word, entered the life of John Leary in a most remarkable way. John is 54 years old and works as a chemist at Eastman Kodak Co., Rochester, New York. He lives in a modest house in the suburbs of Rochester with Carol, his wife of thirty years, and Catherine, his youngest daughter. His other two daughters, Jeanette and Donna, are married and have homes of their own. John has been going to daily Mass since he was seventeen and has been conducting a weekly prayer group in his own home for twenty-four years. For a long time, he has been saying fifteen decades of the Rosary each day.

In April of 1993 he and his wife made a pilgrimage to Our Lady's shrine in Medjugorje, Yugoslavia. While there, he felt a special attraction to Jesus in the Blessed Sacrament. There he became aware that the Lord Jesus was asking him to change his way of life and to make Him his first priority. A month later in his home, Our Lord spoke to him and asked if he would give over his will to Him to bring about a very special mission. Without knowing clearly to what he was consenting, John, strong in faith and trust, agreed to all the Lord would ask.

On July 21, 1993 the Lord gave him an inkling of what would be involved in this new calling. He was returning home from Toronto in Canada where he had listened to a talk of Maria Esperanza (a visionary from Betania, Venezuela) and had visited Josyp Terelya. While in bed, he had a mysterious interior vision of a newspaper headline that spelled "DISASTER." Thus began a series of daily and often twice daily interior visions along with messages, mostly from Jesus. Other messages were from God the Father, the Holy Spirit, the Blessed Virgin Mary, his guardian angel and many of the saints, especially St. Therese of Lisieux. These messages he recorded on his word processor. In the beginning, they were quite short, but they became more extensive as the weeks passed by. At the time of this writing, he is still receiving visions and messages.

These daily spiritual experiences, which occur most often immediately following Communion, consist of a brief vision which becomes the basis of the message that follows. They range widely on a great variety of subjects, but one might group them under the following categories: warnings, teachings and love messages. Occasionally, there are personal confirmations of some special requests that he made to the Lord.

The interior visions contain an amazing number of different pictures, some quite startling, which hardly repeat themselves. In regard to the explicit messages that are inspired by each vision, they contain deep insights into the kind of relationship God wishes to establish with His human creatures. There, also, is an awareness of how much He loves us and yearns for our response. As a great saint once wrote: "Love is repaid only by love." On the other hand, God is not a fool to be treated lightly. In fact, did not Jesus once say something about not casting pearls before the swine? Thus, there are certain warnings addressed to those who shrug God off as if He did not exist or is not important in human life.

Along with such warnings, we become more conscious of the reality of Satan and the forces of evil "...which wander through the world seeking the ruin of souls." We used to recite this at the end of each low Mass. In His love and concern for us, Our Lord keeps constantly pointing out how frail we humans are in the face of such evil angelic powers. God is speaking of the necessity of daily prayer, of personal penance, and of turning away from atheistic and material enticements which are so much a part of our modern environment.

Perhaps the most controversial parts of the messages are those which deal with what we commonly call Apocalyptic. Unusual as these may be, in my judgment, they are not basically any different than what we find in the last book of the New Testament or in some of the writings of St. Paul. After a careful and prayerful reading of the hundreds of pages in this book, I have not found anything contrary to the authentic teaching authority of the Roman Catholic Church.

The 16th Century Spanish mystic, St. John of the Cross, gives us sound guidelines for discerning the authenticity of this sort of phenomenon involving visions, locutions, etc. According to him, there are three possible sources: the devil, some kind of self-imposed hypnosis or God. I have been John's spiritual confidant for over three years. I have tested him in various spiritual ways and I am most confident that all he has put into these messages is neither of the devil nor of some kind of mental illness. Rather, they are from the God who, in His love for us, wishes to reveal His own Divine mind and heart. He has used John for this. I know that John is quite ready to abide by any decision of proper ecclesiastical authority on what he has written in this book

Rev. Leo J. Klem, C.S.B.
January 4, 1996
Rochester, New York

Visions and Messages
of John Leary:

Thursday, July 11, 1996:

After Communion, I could see a casket and a shimmering white light of a spirit rise up from that place. Jesus said: *"My people, you are seeing the fate of everyone as they face the pain of separation of body and spirit. Believe, My friends, that your soul is immortal and will live after the body dies. This is the consequence of original sin, that the body will weaken and decay after death. It is the destination of the spirit that life prepares the way. Those, who are faithful to My Commandments and follow My Will, will receive life everlasting in Heaven. Those, who reject Me, will see their spirit ever suffering the flames of hell and will never see Me again. It is important that people plan their eternal destination, for this is the decision of a lifetime. Do not be taken up with the world so much, that you lose sight of where your soul's spirit will reside. This life is very short. So see that My love reaches out to all and I offer you a glorious feast with Me forever, if you abide by My Will."*

Friday, July 12, 1996:

After Communion, I could see a white Host representing the Eucharist in Holy Communion. It seemed to travel through the darkness with a light showing from it. Jesus said: *"My people, you are seeing how I will be present to you, even during the time of the tribulation. I will not leave My loved ones alone at any time. Even though you may be buffeted by the trial of evil, I will always be there to calm the storm. Look for your strength in My Food from Heaven, the Manna in which you will find My Presence. In the days of the Exodus, I gave the Manna for only bodily nourishment. In the days of the tribulation, I will provide My own body in the Communion that will give you both bodily and spiritual nourishment. All you need do, is pray to Me and ask My help, and I will rush to your aid. If you pray for a spiritual Communion, I will grant you My Physical Presence, which will ward off all the evil spirits. Seek Me in faith and trust and I will provide for all of your needs. Never fear evil, since My power will conquer Satan and his angels and they will be sent to hell."*

Later, I could see some buildings which housed the places of adoration of the Blessed Sacrament. Jesus said: *"My people, treasure all the churches and chapels that keep adoration of My Blessed Sacrament. These quiet places are little jewels of My love, and they hold a special place in My Heart. I am present there waiting to bestow My blessing on every visitor. Everyone, who attends Me in adoration, I give special blessings, since I know you visit Me by a special love of My Presence in My Blessed Sacrament. You come and you are not afraid to give Me part of your precious time on earth. I will remember each of you who are gracious in sharing your love with Me. I love all of My people so much. Why cannot every soul learn to appreciate My treasure in these places? Treasure them now, My people, for soon you shall not have this privilege much longer. Tell everyone where I am present, so others may come and experience your heavenly joy as well."*

Saturday, July 13, 1996:

After Communion, I could see some Arabs and one dressed in a blue turban. Jesus said: *"My people, you wish to find love in this world, but I find more hate. You wish to find peace in this world, but you are at odds with each other. It is the evil one and his fallen angels that are talking in your ears. Do not listen to these spirits of evil, but listen to Me, for I am your source of strength in the darkness. Look to Me for help, for I am your only salvation. As you walk through life and meet many trials, see that I am the light in the darkness. I will lead you if you pray to Me for guidance. Those, who do not seek Me, will truly curse the darkness, for they will find no hope in only their own efforts. See the joy of life ever after lies only with Me and I will answer your every need. Seek My love, and you will find a fulfillment in love as a part of My one Body. If you live loving everyone, you will see the secret of My love in this world."*

Later, I saw a rainstorm and much debris in the streets. Jesus said: *"My people, you will be tested by the weather through fire and water. I have told you these words many times this year, since you are not taking My words seriously. You have seen floods and many violent storms this year. As you look at the debris of damage from this latest storm, let it be a reminder of My words to you. You are seeing the Chastisements come on your land in the areas of greatest sin. Understand, My people, the connection of My Chastisements with the need of reparation for sin. See these happenings as signs which are urging you to convert your life of sin to one of holiness. When enough people pray for sinners and peace in the world, you will see these signs lessen and My joy and love will fill you with My peace."*

Sunday, July 14, 1996:

After Communion, I could see several hills with flames and smoke pouring out of an inferno. Jesus said: *"My people, you are seeing in vision the purification by fire which you have had recently, and you will continue to have in the future. Be forewarned, that many have not heard of My message of conversion, or they have rejected My call. You will have an opportunity for repentance for a time, but this will be short in duration. Shortly after My warning, you must choose between Me or the world. Choose the world, and in a short time it will be thrown on the fire. Choose Me, and you will choose My love and peace forever. As I have told My prophets of old, choose life and you will share in My abundant gifts. This testing by fire will be similar to how metals are purified in the smelting process. Those, who heed My words, will find their everlasting salvation."*

Later, I could see a vision of ships making ready for war or peace keeping. Jesus said: *"My people, I am showing you more preparations for future wars and rumors of wars. For this is how it will be in the End Times. Men have found it difficult to live in peace with each other. Until My reign of peace comes, you will see continuous bickering over land and between old standing enemies. You would think that history should teach you that war has no real winners. Yet, still battles go on, even if men are not successful in their efforts. Pray much, My children, that My peace*

3

will come quickly to end all of this unnecessary strife. Come to your senses My people, and live in peace, or you will live to regret the consequences. Prayer is your way out of all of your problems. Look to Me for your answers, and I will bring peace to all parties. I love you my people, and I want to see you love each other, even your enemies. This is a perfect love I draw all of you to, that you love one an other. Where there is true love, hate and greed will flee and peace will reign."

Monday, July 15, 1996:

After Communion, I could see a little box and it was full of little medals and some of them were blue. Jesus said: *"My people, sacramentals have an important role in the evangelization and conversion of sinners. Many medals of My Mother's various shrines have been struck to be a witness of the blessings given in these holy places. My Mother goes before you to prepare for My Coming again. Listen to her motherly advice as she is with Me always in all she does. Spread the word of her witness by giving out these blessed medals to all who will listen."*

Later, I could see the monstrance and the Host and then I saw a large wagon of fruit and vegetables tip over onto the ground. Jesus said: *"My son, you have learned a lesson in life this day. Understand that the things of this world will be good for you at times, but at other times, as today, there will be misfortunes as well. This is the testing time of life when you must deal with events that have gone awry despite your best efforts. You must restrain your anger and look to Me for help ever more in these situations. Do not worry about the things of this world, but concern yourself more about your behavior and following a good life according to My Will. When you are feeling down, do not despair, but reach out for Me to pick you up again. Do not continue suffering your burden alone, but put it on My back and I will help carry it with you as Simon did for My Cross. Have faith, My children, and look for My love at all times. My blessings go out to all who seek them. Ask My help in your problems and you will see them more resolved with My help than on your own. Have faith in My help and My love and you will witness My peace in all of your affairs."*

Tuesday, July 16, 1996:

After Communion, I could see a light and its base hanging from the ceiling so the light could reach all parts of the room. Jesus said: *"My people, as you place a light in a prominent spot to give the most light on things, let this represent My word as well. I have given My messengers important warnings of the evil age to come. By publication and talks, they are spreading My message of love and My presence among the people. Listen to My words as I prepare you for the test. My prophets have all had to undertake hardship for preaching in My Name. It will be so, even for the prophets of this evil age. If you discern the word given to be true, then see the gift of My love through their words. I love you My people, and I give you My blessings and graces to endure this trial."*

Later, I saw these large buildings in a row next to the street. They could have been government buildings. Jesus said: *"My people, you are saddled with many politicians in your governments. Some have led you well in the forming of your government, but others through the years have abused their power for the wrong reasons. You must pray for your leaders, for they hold much control over you in your electronic age. As the evil age of the tribulation dawns, many such leaders will sell their souls for the greed of power in following the antichrist. Keep far from such people, since they will want to kill the Christians. Pray to Me for help in this dire time, and I will lead you to a safe place away from those wishing to harm you. These things are being told to you, so you will be warned and act accordingly to hide yourself to avoid them."*

Wednesday, July 17, 1996:

At the prayer group, I could see some electrical devices on someone's arm and other signs on their hands. These were the things being used at the Olympics. Jesus said: *"My people, I have told you to watch for the Olympics, where you will see the technology which will lead you to the mark of the beast. These means of buying and selling will soon be implemented for the time of the Antichrist. Do not take the mark of the beast, which may be an electronic chip, even if it means you cannot buy and sell. This will be your sign to go into hiding to avoid the authorities. I will lead you to safety and protect you. Have no fear and rejoice for My victory is not far away."* I could see a TV with a blue picture and suddenly there was a black and white notice across the screen warning to turn it off. Jesus said: *"My people, I have told you at the time of the tribulation to rid yourself of all electronic communications. This is how the Antichrist will hold people in a trance, through hypnotic spells and subliminal messages. Be not afraid of the evil one, but ask for my help at this time and I will provide for your needs."* I could see some troops get out of a truck and they were preparing some detention centers. Jesus said: *"My people, you should be forewarned that various troops, led by the UN, are making ready large detention centers for those who will not accept the new money and food schemes. These men will be the enforcers of the New World Order that will soon be implemented. This will violate your own national government."* I could see Mary come dressed in brown as our Lady of Mount Carmel. Mary said: *"My dear children, I come to give joy and my love to all of my Carmelites and all of my children who wear my brown Scapular. I have given you my promise that if you wear my Scapular and follow my Rosary, you will not face the flames of hell. Give my Scapular to all of your family members and those who want to be saved and I will watch over them. Take advantage of these blessings and you will have nothing to fear in the after life."* I could see a rosary and it was hanging across a scene of a vicious war. Mary came and said: *"My children, you are seeing many wars and violence in your evil age. I beg of you to continue praying your Rosaries as tonight for peace in your world. Prayer is mightier than all the armaments. Seek my help for peace and the conversion of sinners. These two intentions are most important at this critical time for your world."* I could see some leaves as they had fallen from some trees. Jesus said: *"My people, I will tell you now to prepare for some serious events in the fall of this year. Do not concern yourself with dates or be concerned with speculation. I will tell you of these events when you have a need to know about them. Put your faith and trust in Me that I will guard your souls. Come to me often in confession so you may have your soul always in tune with My Will. Be always watchful, for you know not when the thief will come to try and take your soul."* I saw a lot of wood stored and food cartons as well. Jesus said: *"My people, do not be concerned with what you are to eat or wear. Your Heavenly Father watches over the least in His Kingdom. Come to Me and convert your lives. I will forgive your sins and provide for you. Do not be anxious of what you are to store or money to save. Depend on Me for help and not on your own devices. Trust I will provide your food and shelter even throughout the tribulation. I love you My people and My arms await holding all who come to Me."*

Thursday, July 18, 1996:
After Communion, I could see Maria E. and we were praising Jesus in Holy Communion. I then saw some ugly looking birds, as vultures flying over Israel. Jesus said: *"My people, this vision is one of the signs of the End Times when the birds of prey come to Israel. They are coming in anticipation of the great Battle of Armageddon, when they will pick the flesh from those fallen in the final battle of the evil forces. I love you My people and I long to have all of you with Me. Seek Me in prayer and I will guide and protect you in these perilous times. My triumph awaits you as this world's evil age will be coming to a close. Then I will raise up a renewed earth and I will set up My Kingdom on earth under My true peace. All of My faithful will be a witness to these events."*

Friday, July 19, 1996:
After Communion, I could see a vision of a 747 plane and on the side of it was a large plume of fire. Jesus said: *"My people, you have seen a tragic event in this plane's explosion. The vision has shown you the distinctive shape of this plane with a flame to the side. It is unfortunate that certain men have no care for the lives they kill. I have given this to you, that this is indeed a terrorist incident, whether your government will admit it or not. This is another confirmation of the message I gave on increasing terrorist events. There are many evil forces at work which will make such happenings more frequent. As such, innocent lives are taken. Let this be a reminder that there are other children's lives being taken in your daily abortions. Do not forget these innocent lives as well. Pray much for the reparation of the sin in your evil age. My wrath of judgment, by the coming purification, will be the only way that this evil will be brought to its knees. Satan and his angels*

inspire this hate and ruthless killing. Until they are conquered, there will be no peace on the earth. Pray, My children, that this age be shortened to lessen the loss of further souls to hell."

Later, I could see at a distance some fires at night. There were many police and reporters as another serious incident had taken place. It seemed like another plane crash. Jesus said: *"Remember, My people, I have told you, as the End Times approach, you will see many events occur in rapid succession. Each serious incident's occurrence will shock the people at first, but gradually they will wonder what will happen next. It will be this insecure feeling that will raise many fears of the End Times. Have faith and trust in Me, My children, for you will turn to Me for hope and guidance where you are to go to avoid the evil one. The Antichrist's powers will scare many into submission, but you must not give in to his wiles. Remain hidden from him for a short time and you will see how quickly I will subdue him. It will be My victory and triumph over Satan, that all men will look forward to. This will be the time when I will draw all of My faithful close to Me and each will receive their just reward. For those who have received much, much will be expected in return. Go now, My children, and bring as many souls to Me as possible in what ever way you can."*

Saturday, July 20, 1996:

After Communion I could see a small entrance to a cave, and then it opened up into a large room cut out of the rock. There was a tomb along the far wall. Jesus said: *"My people, as once in Rome when My children were persecuted, so you will have to seek underground protection as well. The catacombs hid the bodies of martyrs for My Name. Now, you will see another more evil time, when the men, following the Antichrist, will seek to kill all those who profess My Name. Even those who assist you in hiding will be suspect for punishment. Some will die as martyrs, but I will protect your souls from the evil spirits. Be faithful to My Word and true to My Name and you will soon share with Me in the new Heaven on Earth. You will find salvation with Me no matter what suffering you may have to endure for a while."*

Later, at Dr. Garcia's Grotto Blessing, I saw a large crucifix and it began pulsating and sending out concentric rays of light. I then saw an ethereal white image of Mary looking down on me. Mary said: *"My dear children, I wish to thank you for building this grotto and for your Rosaries this day. You are seeing these pulsations from my Son as you see the pulsations in the miracle of the spinning sun. I bring you to my Son in all I do. I am the mediatrix of all graces and I lead you to your salvation through prayer to follow my Son's Will. When you see me, you see my Son as well. We both welcome you always into our Hearts. Spread our love through your good works to all those around you."*

At Nocturnal Hour, I could see the sun spinning around and it became dark as I saw a whirlpool of evil. Jesus said: *"Some would say, why do I keep giving you messages of the End Times? It is exactly the problem that the people do not want to hear about hard times. They do not even understand that this is a battle between good and evil. If the people cannot see the signs of the End Times, I must keep repeating these messages until they see the true extent evil has come to. It is My love for each soul that drives Me in any way I can to wake up the people and desire conversion. I am truly sending these chastisements because man is in love with himself and his possessions more than Me. When man becomes laid bare of his guilt in My warning, you will see how My mercy is being poured out. Pray much My people and find hope in My purification. Evil's reign is coming to an end when My triumph comes."*

Sunday, July 21, 1996:

After Communion, I could see a young family and I felt a sense of joy in life. Then I saw a Host in a monstrance. Jesus said: *"My people, you should take time to realize how beautiful life can be when you believe and trust in Me. When love is at the center of your life for God and neighbor, all things in life glow with God's handiwork. Everything created is good in itself. It is only when men abuse life and things that evil things come about. If you spend your life working in harmony with My Will, you will witness My peace among you. Pray for those with little or no faith that God may come into their lives to inspire good in their actions."*

(Note: We had brought the monstrance with us to show the priest.)

Later, at St. Joseph's Church, Wayland, after Communion, I kept seeing the Host in the monstrance. There was a feeling to witness the power of the Blessed Sacrament at the talk. Jesus said: *"My son, it is your duty to evangelize My word, since I have given you this mission. It is equally good if you can promote the exposition of My Blessed Sacrament. By your witness of making holy hours before My Blessed Sacrament, you are giving witness of how important it is in your own life. People cannot deny your sincerity in showing your love for Me. This lends further credibility for people to believe in My messages. Continue spreading My Word and remember to continue in asking for the Holy Spirit to guide you what to say. This shows the people that it is not just you who are talking, but that you are asking the Holy Spirit's inspiration."*

Monday, July 22, 1996: (Mary Magdalen feast)
After Communion, I could see a tomb and there was a bright white flash from above. This represented Jesus' Resurrection and when we would be raised as well. Jesus said: *"My dear people, whenever My Resurrection is shared with you, you can see the light of faith give life again to the new body. Your resurrected or glorified bodies will be how I wished all men could be. Adam's sin brought you death, but My Resurrection brings you life. When you are renewed with My peace, you will experience a life of pure love and you will give glory to Me in My everlasting Presence. Your life on earth is but a step in time toward your eternal life with Me. Use your little time wisely in bringing My Word of everlasting life to all who will listen and convert. Give My spark of love to the faithful so they can be an inspiration to their friends and relatives."*

Later, I could see some kingly courts in the time of the tribulation. Then I saw the leaders wearing crowns, and suddenly their crowns were pulled off their heads as they were disposed of. Jesus said: *"My people, your leaders will seek power, so they can help in the alliance with the Antichrist. They will give up their souls for a short earthly fame. As the Antichrist uses these leaders and gains power over their subjects, he will then have these leaders removed and killed. He will do so, so he can have full reign over the world. Just as the evil one's reign becomes worldwide, I will smote him and take his kingdom away. My triumph will come soon after the Antichrist takes power. For the sake of the elect, I will shorten this time of evil and then I will dispatch all of these evil men and evil spirits to hell, never to tempt you again. Then My glory and peace will reign. In a renewed earth I will share My love with My faithful. Continue to pray and prepare for this time. Pray that it comes quickly, so less souls will be lost."*

Tuesday, July 23, 1996:

After Communion, I could see some hats of nurses and then a view of a hospital ward with patients. Jesus said: *"My people, I want you to be a people of service to one another. When you give comfort or help to someone, think as if you are serving Me. For if you serve even the least in My Kingdom, indeed you are serving a part of My Body. When you serve others, you are sharing your gifts and not being selfish with your time. I have asked you to love Me and your neighbor. So when you reach out to help someone, do it for love of Me."*

Later, I could see a large volcano and it was spewing a lot of dark smoke which covered the sun. Jesus said: *"My son, you are seeing a massive volcanic eruption in this vision where dark smoke was evolving. It is true that you will continue to see volcanic eruptions increase, but this one will occur as the comet strikes the earth. There will be a tremendous distortion of the earth's crust which will give rise to many such volcanoes. It will be a combination of these eruptions and the comet's own debris that will give rise to the three days of darkness. Other repercussions will be a changing of the magnetic poles from their present position, and also a brief change in the earth's orbit away from the sun. The gravity of the sun will correct this change in orbit, but for a while the earth will be colder. It is during these three days of darkness that a cave or underground dwelling will afford you the best protection from the cold and the sulfur in the air depleting the oxygen for a short duration. Pray, My people, and listen to My instructions, and I will direct you where to go and how I will feed you with My Heavenly Bread."*

Wednesday, July 24, 1996:

After Communion, I saw some large animals swimming in some swollen rivers. Jesus said: *"My people, you are still seeing some further flooding to come. Some people were loosing their homes, but few consider how the animals' sanctuaries are being lost as well. Man has settled much around the water. So when storms arise, the damage can be extensive. With the increasing storms in your weather, you would do well to live on higher ground away from the water. It would be better for man to manage the land better for when the famines will cause droughts and dust bowls."*

Later, at the prayer group, I could see a plane on fire and then some of the debris under the water. Jesus said: *"My people, I hear many prayer intentions for those that died on this plane crash and for their friends and relatives. I hear your prayer and I will comfort My people. It is good that you see the love of your people for helping those in need. This is another way you can witness to Me in prayer to show those who do not love Me that there are many witnesses to My Word."* I could see several amphitheaters at the Olympics. Jesus said: *"My people, these games can be a powerful focal point for all of the world to love one another and share in respecting each nation who is participating. See your fellow inhabitants of all the earth rely on the same gifts that I share with each of you. A beautiful earth and sky with rain and air to breathe is given you. Many beautiful things are yours if you would look closely at your world as I would see it."* I could see some black people and a thatched roof on a home. Jesus said: *"My people, as you see these games, try and appreciate all that you have and share it with those who are less fortunate. See the beauty in each soul. Each soul is a treasure to Me no matter how little they may have. Live your life for love of Me and love of your neighbor. All sweetness of My glory will come to those who humble themselves and follow My Will."* I could see some men carrying some debris from the plane crash. Jesus said: *"My dear children, while you grieve for those lives lost, a desire goes up among you for justice in this event. I am watching all of your actions and My mercy shines on you, but the reparation for sin is filling My cup of wrath. There will soon be a purification that will bring justice for all the evil that man has committed. See that this evil must be purified since it cries out to heaven that the earth should be made clean."* I could see a picture of the Blessed Mother in flight among a vast crowd of people. Mary said: *"My dear children, I bring my mantle of protection to all of my faith-*

ful. Hear my messages and read again the old messages that you may realize these words of warning and preparation are for your age at this time. My Son has allowed me this time of mercy to wake up the poor souls to seek conversion through my Son's sacraments. Listen to what he tells you as I requested at Cana." I could see some insects and pests devouring your crops. Jesus said: *"My people, you will soon see your crops attacked by various insects and the poor growing weather as well. For a long time you have taken your food for granted. Since I gave you many blessings of rain and fertile soil, you have prospered. As you turn your backs on Me and kill My little ones, you will understand why I am withdrawing these blessings. Pray, My people, for reparation of your sins and you will lessen the severity of these chastisements."* I could see a closed door and it represented the way to our hearts. Jesus said: *"My children, I come knocking on the door of your hearts and souls. As I pursue you to the end of your lives, will you open your hearts to Me? This evil age has hardened many hearts as they trust in themselves more than Me. How long must it take to let you know of My endless love for you? Wake up, My people, before it is too late. Come to Me and I will forgive you of your sins. If you do not open the door to your hearts, I cannot open the Gate to Heaven for you either. My mercy and love awaits you, but you must love Me in return."*

Thursday, July 25, 1996:

After Communion, I could see Maria E. with pain on her face. I then saw a scene in the woods with tree leaves and also some troops in khaki green uniforms searching for people. Jesus said: *"My people, as the tribulation approaches, I will advise you when to go into hiding. Many troops will pursue you into the wilds to torture and kill those in defiance of the Antichrist. Some will be martyred, but I will be looking over you for protection. Some will be promoting My Name even at the risk of being martyred. This ruthless tyranny by the Antichrist and his agents will wake up some of the people who thought this could not happen. Pray much for the wayward souls who are still in need of conversion. I will give everyone ample opportunity to be saved, but each soul has to make their own individual commitment to Me."*

Friday, July 26, 1996:

After Communion, I could see a tall narrow waterfall as at Angel Falls. Jesus said: *"My people, I want you to take time out of your busy days to stop and appreciate the beauty of My creations. You look at the mountains and beautiful falls as in this vision, and your breath is taken away. Yet, I see a beauty in each of your souls which far surpasses any physical beauty of My landscapes. You, too, should appreciate how precious each life is as a gift of My Presence to you, because the Holy Spirit resides in everyone. Even the physical workings of your body is a marvel in every detail. As man tries to fabricate many devices to replace parts of your body, none can compare to that of your original body parts. If I took such care to make such intricate parts of your body, imagine how much I love each soul when that is the most important to Me. Each of you have free will, but I constantly pursue each of you so you can find your divine lover. Look for the beauty most in My love for you and return that love by your faithfulness to My Commandments and following My Will."*

Later, I could see a monstrance and there was a bright light emanating from it. Jesus said: *"My people, see Me in My Blessed Sacrament as a light of faith ready to infuse knowledge of My Loving Heart into all of your hearts. See My deep burning love reaches out for every soul. I pull all of you to myself, since My love calls out to be shared. See in My mercy, a way to reach all of the hearts that are open to My graces. My son, you are going out to all of these talks to proclaim My messages and prepare the people for the tribulation. You go about freely now, but there will come a time when you will be banned from speaking and you will rely on your books to spread the message. As the time of disobedience to My love and My Word becomes more frequent, you will have to move about in secrecy, so the evil ones cannot thwart your mission. Preach My forgiveness of sin in confession and how prayer draws each of you closer to Myself. Keep close to Me in the sacraments, for soon you will have a hard time to find a priest."*

Saturday, July 27, 1996:

After Communion, I could see a road and then I looked down into a sewer. I could see a ferris wheel at an amusement park and a large bomb went off from the sewer raising a big cloud of smoke. Jesus said: *"My people, I have told you how much the evil one hates man. He will inspire man also with hate, enough to bring terror over the entire land. As you witness many of these terrorists' acts, know there are conflicting factions trying to make their importance felt. Get used to hearing of these events, since their frequency and severity will increase. Ruthless men are staging these acts in protest of your government's actions. This rivalry between the Jews and the Arabs will precipitate many problems, because of your government's support of Israel. Pray for peace in your world before this will consume you. I am coming to rid the world of the evil spirits and the evil men. Your world will be in such chaos, that you will welcome My purification and peace with open arms. Pray this time will be shortened for the sake of the elect."*

Later, at Nancy Donohue's house, Oneonta, N.Y., during the rosary, I could see some statues and a picture of the hearts of Jesus and Mary on the wall. Jesus said: *"My people, you are seeing the faithful in a prayer group in this vision. It would be good if you could join a prayer group or start one of your own. This practice builds up the people in their faith, and also helps in the reparation for the sins of the world. As time draws closer to the tribulation, your prayer groups will take on a new meaning as the early Christian meetings. The Mass will be scarce to find, so your prayer groups will be a method of uniting My people. Still further on, you may have to flee into hiding, but your prayer members will now help each other with My help to take care of your needs. During the coming years, you will see how much prayer and trust in My Word will be all that you will have to rely on. See My love and mercy are coming to purify the earth and renew it. Live in faith for the day I will invite you to My Heaven on Earth."*

Sunday, July 28, 1996:

At St. Mary's, Oneonta, N.Y., after Communion, I was moving down the aisle of a Church as the priest was greeting the people. Several of the people seemed aloof and did not want to listen to the Gospel message. Jesus said: *"My son, I am thankful for your efforts in evangelizing My people by conversion to Me and away from their worldly ways. I have, indeed, given you many mes-*

sages which may be difficult to understand for some. In all of what I do, man must realize My ways are not your ways. See that My love for man is the basis for all I am doing, to make you aware of the evil age you are in. Do not be confused by details or doubt by people's questions. Realize these messages are given to bring man to an appreciation of his purification before his entry into heaven. I know you would die for My Name and you will not disbelieve anything I have told you. Be calm and peaceful in all of your presentations and be ready to help those understand My ways. Ask the people to pray quietly for discernment in how I will lead each person to their salvation. My sacraments and your prayers are your strengths to know and love Me. Keep your focus on Me in all of your life and I will provide for all of your needs."

Later, at Fonda, N.Y., before the Blessed Sacrament I had a vision of an Indian maiden. I had asked the Lord to allow her to give a message. Kateri said: *"My dear son, you have prayed properly in asking for Fr. Luke's cure, that it be according to the will of Jesus and in His Name. I can pray and intercede with my loving Jesus, but Jesus is the one who would allow a cure. Ask Jesus in faith for a cure, and he will give you an answer. Continue to pray for this intention, for Fr. Luke is doing a wonderful work in his life. Remember, also, your intention for your daughter whom I am still watching over at your request. Thank you for coming to my memorial place, for you truly have faith in the power of prayer and my intercession."*

Monday, July 29, 1996: (St. Martha)

After Communion, I could see Jesus suffering on the cross and my focus came in close to see the crown of thorns and how He suffered from it. Jesus said: *"My people, I want you to know how much I suffered for you on the Cross, especially, as you see from this crown of thorns. I have given you an example that your life will be one of suffering also. Everything in this world you must struggle for and that includes your spiritual life as well as your physical life. You need to work for a living and use your hands for good works. Yet, you need a firm prayer life and my help for you to survive in your spiritual life as well. You need to work at both lives if you are to survive and reach your destination with Me. Come to Me in all of your efforts. I will give you rest from your work. You will suffer much in this life, but your crown of sainthood awaits you, when you have accomplished all I have intended for each of My faithful."*

Tuesday, July 30, 1996:

At St. Andrew's Church near Allentown, Pa., I saw an outline of a place where a statue of Our Lady was, but now it was empty. Mary came and said: *"My dear children, you have received many of my messages from various visionaries, and still you are looking for more messages. I have come to you as John the Baptist prepared the people for my Son's First Coming. I am bringing you close to me and in turn close to my Son, since our hearts are as one. You have heard John the Baptist say: 'I must decrease while He increases.' this is why I have shown you in many visions how I am not being seen as well. Many visionaries have stopped receiving messages from me. You will see my Son, Jesus, come with messages for some, more than myself. I will still watch over you with my mantle, but the messages will be waning. See in this event, that my love is not leaving, but the End Times are growing closer. I love you my children. Continue with your Rosaries and devotions for the conversion of sinners and peace in your world. Love is lacking in many souls. Ask my Son to come to their hearts and his grace will touch those open to believe."*

Later, at St. Andrew's Church near Allentown, Pa., I could see some poles with telephone lines. I then saw a roof with several sets of eyes looking toward me. Jesus said: *"My dear people, I love you and do everything to bring you close to Me. Listen to My words of the Gospel and live them in all you do. Be an example of My love to everyone. In your vision you are seeing how many will be watching your every move. There will be some evil men determined to seek out Christians for torture. This is a warning as I gave before, that you be careful in your communications. Others are listening on phones and electronically for those to keep records on as a threat to the Antichrist. Be watchful and protect yourself by other means of communication. Go My people and be at peace and I will watch over you."*

Wednesday, July 31, 1996: (St. Ignatius of Loyola)

After Communion, I could see a priest saying Mass. Jesus said: *"My people, you have much to be thankful for in your order priests. Many missionaries and teachers have resulted from their founders. These founders were men of vision for making a better world. Give praise and glory to god for all the inspirations given these priests and brothers. They have continued and have enhanced the faith of many of My faithful. All of you should take a lesson from their dedication to help others. See in their example a means to perpetuate the faith into future generations. All of those who are baptized should help pass on the faith to their younger members. It is by spreading My Gospel that more can hear My Word and be saved. It is your soul's desire to be with Me, that will bear fruit, and allow you to reach your salvation by believing in Me and accepting Me into your lives."*

Later, at the prayer group, I could see some buildings with red bricks as in a city and there was a stoplight in the green position. Jesus said: *"My son, you are truly being called to evangelize My people before and during the tribulation. I have asked you to lead souls to Me and you have been following My Will to go forth. I have given you a hard message of warning to the people, much like I gave to Jonah. Be faithful, My son, and I will lead you where to go and what to say. You will not travel very long during the tribulation and I will bring this evil to an end."* I could see a light with some people in fear of the horrible events going on around them. Jesus said: *"My people, as you see the events I have warned you about to happen, many will be fearful of what will take place. I have given you, My son, My peace amidst all of this strife. You are to continue being a beacon of hope for the people and encourage them to have faith and trust in My protection."* I could see a man dressed as a wizard or someone in the occult. Jesus said: *"My people, do not be misled by evil spirits and false witnesses who will show marvels and evils of magic. Have no fear of what they can do to the body. Fear only the wicked who can tempt your soul to leave Me and worship the evil one. Pray much, My people, and rely on your weapons of crosses, rosaries and holy water in fighting the evil spirits. Have faith and I will deliver you from the grips of the evil ones."* I could see a room with many newsreels, where there was a lot of splicing of films. Jesus said: *"My people, I am warning you about the printed word in your media. There are many well meaning people involved with the media, but in the last analysis, there are a few controlling what gets printed and how it is presented. Know that this is being controlled and do not believe all that is portrayed. If you seek the truth, follow My Word and I will show you the way to Heaven."* I could see a wall with barbed wire and there were many people placed in a detention center. Jesus said: *"My people, you are seeing how some will be imprisoned for not following the authorities in taking the mark of the beast. Those, who defy the authorities, will be tortured and abused and some even martyred. This is why going into hiding, under My protection, will be more favorable than open defiance. Some of My faithful will continue evangelizing, as yourself, but these will be directing My people until they are silenced."* I could see some men marching in the army. Mary showed me this vision and she said: *"My dear children, I call on you to observe how man relies on his armaments and armies for his security. How the evil one has deceived you into taking trust in yourselves, instead of trust in God. History has shown you how unreliable it is to depend on arms. I am telling you, my children, to choose Jesus as your security. He is the one who will save you. Open your heart to His graces and He will show you the way to save your soul."* I could see a crucifix leading me through various lands. Jesus said: *"My son, there are various healing ministries which I call My children to. See that when I healed someone, I healed their sins first and then the sicknesses of the body. You, too, must do likewise. Seek to heal the person's rejection of God first. Evangelize their souls first, then they will be open to the proper disposition of accepting a bodily healing through faith in Me. Without faith, bodily healings will be difficult."*

Thursday, August 1, 1996:
   After Communion, I could see Maria E. with her eyes closed giving praise to God. I then saw a cart with packs of butter and other food commodities. Jesus said: *"My dear people, as you draw closer to the End Times, you will see signs of the coming famine. Already, many of your farmers are meeting with hard times. There will be difficulties in growing crops, since some areas will have*

drought while others will have too much rain and not enough sun. As these conditions grow worse, it will tax your food stores. Not enough people are farming to provide all that is needed. I am warning your countries now to prepare for this problem in their future planning or more will die from starvation. Pray My people to have the strength to endure these trials."

Friday, August 2, 1996:

After Communion, I could see a car with its headlights on at night as if searching. Then I saw the water from under the sea and I was looking up. Jesus said: *"This stiff necked people of your day are very much like those that greeted Me. I came to them with the Gospel and preached to them in parables, but they did not hear and understand. I performed miracles of healing for them to see, but they did not see and understand the meaning to be cured spiritually and physically. It will be the same for all of My prophets and messengers. For those in your day, who do not hear the messages and take them to heart, they will be wanting in the Last Days. Again, they will see miracles of healings and the signs of the End Times, and still some will not believe. It is only when people admit they need conversion from their sins, that my graces will work in their heart for salvation. You can plead with these obtuse spirits to repent day and night, but if they refuse the grace of My inspiration, they will not be saved. It is important, therefore, to pray for these lost souls, to have their hearts open to change. If they do not change their ways, then truly they will be deaf and blind to My words of freedom in the spirit and will be lost forever."*

Later, I could see a large cross representing Jesus' dying on the cross. Then I saw many smaller crosses as well. Jesus said: *"My son, you are seeing how I gave up My life freely, that man's sins would be forgiven, and that all men will be open to gaining heaven. By this act I am witnessing My love for all of you. As this age comes to an end, you will see evil appear to gain in strength. There will be some willing to defend My Name with their lives as well. I have already prepared you, that you may encounter serious opposition in defending My Word in the messages. I will go before you and guide you in this battle. You will have to give witness to My love and your lack of fear in defending Me. Your work will continue into the tribulation, so you can proclaim My messages for those to repent, before Satan steals their hearts. Pray much, My children, for all of you must suffer in some way to claim your crown by being faithful to My Word. Those, who follow Me even amidst adversity, will receive a prophet's reward."*

Saturday, August 3, 1996:

After Communion, I could see a valise of money and then a woman's purse. Jesus said: *"My dear people, money of itself is not evil, but craving it in all of its forms for its own sake can be sinful. Do not be concerned for what you will eat or wear, for the worldly seek these things only. At the same time, do not put your trust in the security of money or treat it as a god. Elusive wealth will never give you peace or security. Those with little money, constantly seek it or steal it, while those with money are seeking nervously to preserve it. I tell you, that you must place your trust and security with Me, for My help is everlasting. You think with enough money, you will have peace, but you will be disturbed by many wanting to steal it. Instead, seek your peace from Me and I will satisfy your soul. As in the scriptures, you cannot have two masters. You will either love Me or love the money of the world. You cannot love Me and money. Those, who follow Me and ask for perfection, must seek to sever all ties to their possessions. Seek Me first, and you need not worry, for I will provide for you."*

Later, before the Blessed Sacrament, I saw the Host in a monstrance and there was a flame spinning around as the spinning sun. I saw some angels kneeling in adoration. Jesus said: *"My people, I bring you the three questions I asked Peter: 'Do you love Me?' if you love Me, then tell Me over and over in your own words. I wish to hear from all of My people how much they love Me. Every day when you greet Me, you can tell me that you love Me and repeat it as often as you like. In this way, you can show Me your love in your words, in your prayers, and in your good deeds. I love you all with an infinite, unconditional love. I will love you until your dying day even if you offend Me often. I have given you the grace of confession to have your sins forgiven. Each time you start with a clean soul again, as a witness to the glory of My One Body. As you sin, you fall away from Me gradually, but when you are forgiven, I welcome you back to My loving communion of Saints. Do everything for love of Me and you will be on your way to perfecting your love. When you are judged, I will ask again how did you love Me and your neighbor. Your response will be your judgment.*"

Sunday, August 4, 1996:

After Communion, I saw Jesus standing in His crown of thorns suffering for us. Jesus said: *"My people, you have seen how I fed the multitudes from the few fish and barley loaves. This is an example of how I shower everyone with many blessings and graces. No one can say they have not received My help. As in the scriptures: 'To one who receives much, much will be expected.' as I have given you gifts in money and health, so you should consider sharing these gifts with your neighbor. Do not be selfish in your possessions, but be willing to help those in need. I have told you many times: 'Whatever you do for the least in My Kingdom, you do it for Me.' it is not enough for you to say, 'Lord, Lord.' whatever you say with your lips, you must apply in how you live each day. So if I come to you begging for food or money, do not be quick to reject Me. See My presence in each person and pour out your love on My children in whatever way you can help them. Some may ask your prayer help. Be ready to go the extra mile in receiving those who come to you. By helping those in need, you store treasures up in Heaven which no one can steal nor will they be forgotten. I wish that all of My people would be willing to sacrifice some for each other. Then your world would experience My peace in more abundance. Learn this lesson of sharing the gifts you have been given, and your life will come closer to following My Will, where I ask a total abandonment of all that is worldly."*

Later, I could see three hearts joined together. Jesus said: *"This vision, My people, is to prepare you for the significance of My Transfiguration. Both Elijah and Moses were taken up into Heaven. You should realize that Elijah's messages very much taught of the evils going on in his day. Again, Moses brought My people away from Egypt into the dessert. Through faith and trust in Me, I provided food and water to My people. There are many parallels of these things to the experiences you will see in the future. When the tribulation comes, the people will have to place their trust in Me that I will provide water and the Heavenly Manna. The messages, I am giving you, are very much like the future events Elijah foretold. All of these examples are showing you My plans are always being fulfilled. Listen to My words of warning, and you will be ready to share in the beauty of the second coming. Those, who have faith, will be protected and provided for."*

Monday, August 5, 1996:
After Communion, I was looking down on a pool table as a game of chance. Jesus said: *"My son, you have seen today in the Old Testament, how there were false prophets in years gone by. Those false prophets are soon found out as they are not in My favor and they are as fortune tellers, predicting the future by chance. You discern those false witnesses, by their fruits and how they do not receive My blessings. Those who are true to My Word, and follow My calling, I will give testimony to the truth of their fruits. Look for love in the hearts of My witnesses versus the opportunity and fame sought by the false prophets. Wherever I raise up My prophets to speak to you, Satan will also try to deceive you in the false witnesses. Discern this deception through prayer and look for My favor on those following My Will. My true prophets follow Me in a proper life and are full of My hope and peace. My love inspires their hearts and My hand is before them."*

Later, I saw a metal cross and it began to bend on one side. Then I saw a white rose in a vase standing all alone at night. Jesus said: *"My people, I show you My Cross, that you may carry your own Cross to your destiny with Me in Heaven. If you follow My ways and remain open to My direction, I will be able to mold you into following My Will for you. This is why you see the Cross bending, as I will shape your life until it is more pleasing to Me. In the second vision, you see the white rose which symbolizes My love and peace that I am willing to share with all who come to Me. When you experience My peace, this is the peace that I wish the whole world could make its own. My love goes to your every last fiber so that all of you becomes a part of Me. This love and peace I give you, you must share with all of My people. If you could only dwell on these thoughts of My blessings, many would be drawn to Me and your soul would desire nothing else. Pray, My children, for an understanding of My ways and you will transform your earthly life into a heavenly life. Remain close to My Heart and I will give you My peace and love at all times."*

Tuesday, August 6, 1996: (Transfiguration)

After Communion, I saw some atom bomb explosions on the commemoration of Hiroshima. Jesus said: *"My people, while some are in a festive mood with My mountaintop experience, others are remembering the deaths in a war gone by. This vision of atomic weapons you have seen several times. It still poses a threat over your world which is full of hate in various places. Peace in your world is a delicate balance, while men's hearts are still far apart from each other. I tell you many times to pray for peace, since man is very close to causing some catastrophic wars with these weapons. With so much hate in men's hearts, and not enough love, the evil one will have his influence and war could turn more serious. Pray much for your leaders, that your anger may not create your own chastisement on the world."*

Later, I could see a woman come towards me dressed in a black robe. Jesus said: *"My dear son, many times I have told you when souls are saved, you will have to bear the burden of harassment and misunderstanding. No matter how clear you try to speak, there will still be some left in confusion. Even though you may encounter difficulties, continue to speak in My Name with authority, so the people will hear My Word, and My love will touch their hearts. You are only asked to be My instrument in doing nothing more than your duty. Be privileged to be able to speak out for souls that need conversion. Preach My forgiveness in confession, and the tenderness of My love which awaits My faithful before the Blessed Sacrament. It is the example that you set, as well as the messages, that will influence souls. Pray much, My child, for each group you meet, that their souls and hearts will be open to Me, through the power of the Holy Spirit, in you. You will also need prayers of protection wherever you go, since the evil one will try desperately to stifle your work. Continue to follow My Will, and your reward will be to see those souls turned from their ways to My ways."*

Wednesday, August 7, 1996:

After Communion, I could see a stand up dresser for clothes. Jesus said: *"My people, as you awake each day, think of Me even as you ready yourself for the day. In the vision you are seeing a dresser. When you put on your clothes, put on My heartfelt mercy, and live My Gospel, as you make the things of this life a part of your life. If you live your life in Me, you will follow Me as a second nature. Always remember to pray for My help. I ask you for your allegiance, so you will recognize Me as the master of your life each day. I walk beside you each day, and I share your joys and difficulties as well. Look to Me for help in all you do, for I am always close by, if you would reach out to Me in your need. You have My assurance that you will never be tested beyond your endurance in faith. Come to Me and you will find your rest. I give My graces freely to all who seek them."*

Later, at the prayer group I saw a young boy watching the Olympic games with an aspiration to one day being such an athlete. Jesus said: *"My people, as you aspire to do great physical feats, I draw your attention to spiritual aspirations as well. As you admire runners for their quickness, look at the Saints whom you should admire, for their virtues of patience and perseverance in the faith. Many lessons in your spiritual life can be had by following the lives of the saints. These men and women should be your true heroes."* I could see a water barrel with its precious life giving water. Jesus said: *"My people, in some areas you have an abundance of fresh water. Over time, you will see water becoming more important, especially in areas of drought. Even the salt water will begin to spoil your fresh water. Water is a precious gift and a necessity in life. See to it that you are thankful for all the gifts you have, even those you do not fully treasure."* I could see some cupboards where food was stored. Jesus said: *"My people, you will witness a growing famine over the land as the tribulation time approaches. For a time, it would be advisable to have at least one year's supply of food in storage. Later, there will be riots and people will be searching all over for food to steal. When life is severe, you will then need to flee the cities, but up to that time, you may require the food you have stored. If all the people saved extra food, there would not be so much chaos."* I could see some large food factories. Jesus said: *"My people, I am warning you, when you see only a few people controlling your food sources, the evil men will use contrived food shortages to control the people. This will tighten the supplies of food available, so only the mark of the beast will be allowed to buy it. This again is why My faithful should store extra food now."* I could see Our Lady holding the baby Jesus and showing me some aborted fetuses. Mary said: *"My dear children, look in your world how your world has little respect for life in the womb. Do not fail to voice your opinion against those who would allow this killing to continue. My Son is most displeased with this sin in your land, and many have ignored such killing that goes on. If you wish to show your fervent love for me, reach out in prayer and action to fight this evil in your land."* I could see a huge ship at night and there was a bright light in front of it showing the way. Jesus said: *"My people, see this ship as your country, when it first was formed and followed a great faith in Me. This light of faith is slowly being snuffed out by your separation of church and state. Love of Me is given lip service and not truly as I desire how you should live. If My light goes out, your ship will travel aimlessly in the night. Wake up your people to its lack of faith in Me, so you will light your way. Without Me, you will be lost in your own sins of darkness."* I could see someone hanging out their wash to dry on some lines. Jesus said: *"My people, you will have a slow change in your style of living, as various problems will lower your standard of living. As people have less, you will have to adjust in coping with your new circumstances. See this as a blessing, so you will come to depend on Me more than yourselves for your needs. I will help you and lead you if you would have trust and faith in My aid."*

Friday, August 9, 1996:

After Communion, I could see a grave site ready to receive a casket. Then I saw the casket being lowered into the ground. Jesus said: *"My people, I bring you this vision, that you may never forget the mortality of the body, and the immortality of the soul. Whenever you see a funeral, think of the day when you also will face the judgment. I love you, My people, and I am ever present to you. Do not take comfort in the possibility of conversion to-*

morrow, when you can do it today. Take care of your soul every day and be ever watchful, for you know not when I come. Love Me each day, and strive to be close to the one who desires you to be with Me. I am so willing to bring all of My souls to Heaven, if they would only make an effort to love their Lord. You see how quickly life passes before you. Make the best of your time for prayer and good deeds, and you will have stored treasure in Heaven, far surpassing anything you could have on earth."

Later, I could see some cartoons on TV. Jesus said: *"My people, I wish to give a message for protecting My little ones. Too often in your society of electronics, you have allowed the TV to become your babysitter. Many children are watching programming without any care from their parents as to what they are viewing. Most of the cartoons and some other programs are not proper example · to impressionable young children. Know exactly what your children are watching or leave the TV turned off. Even in the cartoons there is much violence and poor moral character portrayed. You want to teach your children good morals, since you are responsible for their spiritual training. See to it that your children have only good influences around them, or you may not understand how they can turn so violent. If they are taught violence and are around violence in the home, this may form deep effects on their future behavior. Pray with your children, and bring them up in the faith by your own instruction. When you face Me on judgement for how you fared with your children, you can stand proud that you did your best. If you fail to teach them properly, then you will face the weight of that judgment against you."*

(Note: News broke at 10:00 p.m. of the suspected killer of Kali Poulton.)

Saturday, August 10, 1996:

After Communion, I could see a sandbox and there were no children in it. Jesus said: *"My people, I remind you of how much love I have for My little ones. I have told you in the scriptures that for those who bring harm to My little ones, it is better to have a millstone placed about their neck, and they be thrown into the sea. This injustice in the killing of My little ones demands much reparation for this sin. There is even more judgement coming, since you do not even recognize the evil in your daily abortions. Once life is set in motion, it is precious and should be protected in all of its forms. When you violate My creations, you demand punishment from My justice. My mercy of forgiveness awaits all sinners, if they choose to convert, but there still remains the reparation of this sin, either by suffering on earth or in purgatory. Those evil doers, who do not repent, will be cast into the eternal flames of my wrath in hell."*

Later, I could see a large circle with many lights as the warning. Then I could see myself moving through tunnels underground. Jesus said: *"My people, many times I have advised you to seek out caves for protection from the evil men, during the tribulation. Some have scorned this message from their pride and their fear. You know how much I love you and that I would not mislead you. If you doubt My words on the caves, then I call on you about the cure of Naaman's leprosy. (4 Kings:5) the prophet (Eliseus) told him to cleanse himself seven times in the Jordan river. At first Naaman refused, but later he was convinced by his servant to do as the Lord requested through the prophet. He was then healed. So in your case, I give you another reason to follow Me to the caves, since it is the best place for your protection, and because I have said it. Believe in Me and follow My Word, and you will see how My love will be poured out in your protection. Follow Me wherever I lead you, and you will never go wrong. I will see to all of your needs, if you would just be faithful in loving Me."*

Sunday, August 11, 1996:

After Communion, I could see several people kissing and coming together. Jesus said: *"My people, I love you and I wish you would love Me and each other. I come to give a message of hope to all those who are married or are seeking marriage. You are in an age where individual comfort and convenience runs your lives. My friends, love in marriage is the image I give you for understanding the love between man and Myself. Perfect love comes only when you give of yourself to the other person. If you expect a marriage to last, it must be with My help and your commitment to that covenant in keeping it alive. When selfishness enters in or you no longer feel committed to the covenant of the marriage*

bond, this is where trust is lost. *If you cannot commit your life to doing everything for the other person ahead of your own desires, then you are not ready for marriage. Keep your communication open to Me and your partner and you will preserve your bonds. Offer to do things for each other as a way of enriching your love. Marriage is a beautiful love of making your lives a part of each other. It is too precious to lose this relationship. Do everything in prayer and friendship possible to keep couples together. Remember that this union is a Blessed Sacrament and My way of giving you of Myself. Give of yourself with My loving help and your marriages will be preserved."*

Later, at Muriel Trunfio's house, during the Rosary, I at first saw Our Lady holding Jesus as an infant. I then saw a large dove and all around the outside of the dove were small dark circles with faces. These circles represented the souls in mortal sin living now. The Holy Spirit said: *"I am the Spirit of Love and I come to this group to remind you of My presence you have witnessed in the dove in Betania and the miracle pictures in the collage. I know you all are deeply committed to prayer, and I bring you a mission that all of you can help with. Many pray for the souls in purgatory. This is a noble cause, but you are seeing the most serious cause is those lost souls who still have a chance to be saved. Pray in earnest for those souls away from God. I am present in all of them, and I need your help to sway them from their earthly ways. You, also, can affect those souls in your family. I know all souls have free will, but you are even more responsible to continue witnessing and praying for those souls in your own family. Do not rest until they have been won over to God. I will strengthen you in this battle of good and evil, so that you may have perseverance to the end in saving souls. Never forget for one day, to continue in this task to save souls living now, since time is running out for their conversion. Your guilt for not working harder will be even worse after the judgement. So do all you can do now, and you will one day rest in My Kingdom, justified that you did all in your power to help save these souls."*

Later, I could see long rows of new buildings being constructed to hold people in detention centers. Jesus said: *"My people, I have warned you to prepare for the tribulation, which is not far off. You are seeing, in the vision, how the evil men are planning the control of large groups of people. They are now building detention centers to house many people. See, My friends, that they intend to use these facilities when they try to force the mark of the beast on everyone. Those, who refuse to recognize the UN troops as the current authority to run the One World government, will be placed in these camps to break their resistance. You will see, My friends, that it is better to seek Me in the refuges or caves than to fight the authorities. Those outlawed, for not fol-*

lowing the Antichrist, will be tortured and imprisoned in these camps. You will see that it is better to be free trusting in Me, than to defy the agents of evil by yourself. Pray for the strength to discern how I will lead you during this time."

Monday, August 12, 1996:

After Communion, I could see some flames and black smoke from a forest fire. Jesus said: *"My people, as you see the flames from out west and the rumbling volcanoes, you are seeing the beginnings of My purification of the earth. Many evils have befallen your world and instead of getting better, your sins are worsening. This cannot go on without some retribution. Your world in its evil is beyond repair. It will take a massive purification to eradicate this evil. The demons and evil men must be vanquished, as you will see in the not too distant future. By purifying the earth, I will be making it ready for my promise of an era of peace, free from evil. Keep your faith and trust in me, and soon you will see these events come to fruition."*

Later, at Our Lady of Lourdes I could see a baby dead after birth. Jesus said: *"My people, I wish to instruct you in how to deal with those able to understand the issue of abortion. Many times I have asked you to pray for these potential mothers, that they see the value and preciousness of life far and above any reason to destroy even one life. So, also, you must deal with those that may not desire an abortion, but they are tolerant of women who wish to kill their growing babies. Think of how abhorrent it was for a woman to drown her children and how she was tried for murder. Is it any less serious at which point in life that someone would take a life? All life is precious to Me whether it be an adult or a growing baby in the womb. If you could prevent someone from committing murder, would you not do it, no matter whether you would offend people's feelings or not? It is important, My friends, to advise your people that if your abortions are not stopped, My hand of wrath will come upon you. Remind them of My justice with Noah, Sodom and Gomorrah, and Niniveh. You will meet a similar fate, unless you fight against this killing. Do not allow the evil one a victory in your killings because you were too lazy or afraid to stand up for my commandments against murder."*

Tuesday, August 13, 1996:

After Communion, I could see a green leaf and then some hay being harvested. Jesus said: *"My people, I am calling you to the harvest of souls, while you still experience the time of My mercy. There will come a time when men's hearts will be hardened, and evil will thwart conversions during the tribulation. Realize, My friends, that your evil age needs conversion now more than ever, since your time for conversion grows short. As you see the nights get longer, you know winter is coming. Hark to the signs of the End Times, for you need to repent before it is too late. My mercy abounds now, so take advantage of this grace while you have it at your service."*

Later, I saw the outside view of a landing space shuttle. Jesus said: *"My son, you have received many messages, and it is your mission to share them with the people. Since this subject of reincarnation has come before you, I will tell you why I have not mentioned this before. Reincarnation back into bodies in your time does not happen as some would propose. I have given you nothing on this subject because it does not exist. Returning in glorified bodies, that are perfect in every way, will happen one day at the judgement. Do not be misled on these subjects, for all you are to know, I have revealed to you in My Scriptures. If I have not taught it, then it is not necessary for your salvation. If reincarnation existed, everyone would have experienced it and not just a few. This view gives an impression that you may not have to worry how you will face the judgement. Anything, which misleads you from the truth, is from the evil one. Do not concern yourself with this misbelief, but instead seek to be perfect in the one soul and one life you are given. By loving Me and following my will, you will reach heaven by faith in my word and My grace in the salvation I have bought for you on the Cross."*

Wednesday, August 14, 1996:

At the prayer group, I could see people sitting on little stools praying the rosary. Mary came and said: *"My dear children, I am happy to greet all of you tonight. I thank you for offering up all of your Rosaries for my intentions. My Rosary is your weapon against evil in the world. Make it a practice in your life to say my Rosary*

J. TereLyn.

every day to keep you close to my Son and to help atone for the reparation of much sin in the world." I could see St. Therese come as a nun. She said: *"I thank you for witnessing to my messages as yesterday. I wish you all would see how serious it is to pray for the conversion of sinners. Lost souls may have a change in their lives through your intercession of prayer. Never give up on saving souls. There is nothing more valuable an activity in your world than to work to save souls. Since I have come to Heaven, I have never ceased struggling in this battle for souls. See the importance of this work and lead souls by your example."* I could see a women dressed in black as Mother Cabrini. She said: *"I am sorry that you could not make it to my shrine this year. God willing, it may still not be too late. Encourage all souls to come to my well of healing waters. Remember my example in helping the poor whenever you can. These works of mercy are what Jesus asks of you each day in caring for his Mystical Body."* I could see some nuns teaching and caring for the sick. Jesus said: *"My people, do not forget that women have an important role in My Church. Over the years, the orders of nuns have been faithful in teaching and nursing. Many have to thank them for their religious upbringing. As the nuns in some areas have declined in numbers, I must call on the lay women, especially mothers, to insure their children are taught the faith that you treasure so much. It is important to pass this gift of My Word on to the future generations. See how My Mother helped in My upbringing as your model."* I could see some priests teaching the children. Jesus said: *"My friends, I bring to your attention how you should be thankful for your order priests as missionaries and teachers of My Word. You have witnessed many of the saints who have founded such societies for the benefit of all men. Give thanks for the lives of these founders, and the priests who have joined these orders."* I could see some large buildings which housed the Olympics. Jesus said: *"My people, I wish to remind you of the Olympics I warned you about earlier. It is unfortunate that the terrorists have used this event to mark their evil deeds. These events of terror will continue. I also wish to point out how new means of buying and selling were introduced at these Olympics, especially the smart card I have warned you about. These devices are being trial runned for now, but soon they will be forced on you to accept them.*" I could see some men wearing crowns as of praise. Jesus said: "*My people, even though it is good to seek your accomplishments in this world, keep them in perspective that you do everything for Me. When you do things for yourself, your worldly glory will dissipate quickly. When you do things for My glory, then your graces will be stored in Heaven. When you do things for Me in secret, I will reward that person more. Someone, who seeks praise for making great displays for Me in front of men out of pride, will have their reward here. I need all of My faithful to give good example in their prayer lives by being humble and vigilant.*"

Thursday, August 15, 1996: (Assumption of Mary)
After Communion, I had a sense of Maria E.'s presence but I could only see a black box. I then saw a close up picture of Mary wearing a crown and a sense of being at the Dormition Abbey in Jerusalem. Mary said: "*My dear children, this feast celebrates my physical joining of my Son in Heaven. Since His birth, our hearts have been as one. You have seen by my 'yes' to the angel, that my mission of being Jesus' mother was fulfilled. I have, since that moment at the bottom of the Cross, been your mother as well through St. John. I mention these things, because all of my children have been given a mission by God, both in the physical world by your talents and the in the spiritual world by your graces. Come to my Son and pray to Him, so he will enlighten each of you to see your mission on the earth. Ultimately, you are on your way home to Him in Heaven by this path, but you are drawn to help others as well. Continue your prayer life with both of us at your side, and you will one day be joined with us in Heaven on your resurrection day.*"

Friday, August 16, 1996:
After Communion, I saw an angel flying with large wings. I asked Jesus permission for my angel Mark to give the message. Mark said: "*I stand before God, and I am happy to give a message which I have not done for a long time. You have recognized my work in helping you daily and I will honor your requests. You are seeing also, the importance of your mission in saving souls at this time. See to it that you guard yourself at all times, since many are watching your behavior as an example. Keep working hard*

to get out these precious messages, that are God's gifts to you and the people. Be ever thankful to God for each message, and keep up your prayer life as central, if they are to continue. The Lord has seen fit to use you as his instrument. Do everything in your power to be worthy of that grace. It is indeed a gift, but one that must be guarded and cared for with love for Him."

Later, I could see Pope John Paul II and he was looking back at someone behind him. His hair was white and he looked stressed over what was going on around him. Jesus said: *"My son, I have shown you this vision of the Pope once before. You are seeing the signs of his struggle with those around him that are trying to remove him from the papacy. My mother will watch over him as he will lead the Remnant Church after the schism in the Church. The Pope's destruction is being sought, but these men will not be able to kill him. Prepare, My people, when this split will again attack My Church. Satan will be given a short time to test men's faith. You will see this replacement of the Pope, called the little horn of the Apocalypse, bring apostasy and blasphemy to My Church. He will misdirect even some of the elect. Remain faithful to My teachings of the faith and reverence John Paul II as my true Pope for this age. See when another pope takes power, that he will mislead the people. Do not recognize him as authentic, since he will be an imposter pope. In everything, follow My Word from the scriptures and do not be misled by bishops and priests who teach heresies as dogma. Pray for My help and I will give discernment to all who ask it of Me."*

Saturday, August 17, 1996:

After Communion, I could see a wooden casket during the time of the tribulation. Jesus said: *"My people, during the end times, death will be all around you. Pray for My protection in those days and I will come to your aid. You will see many hardships from diseases and food shortages in the famine. I have asked you to pray and My angel will deliver you my heavenly Manna for food. There will be healers among you who will help with many diseases. Still further, you will see death in wars and killings by looters. Near the end of the tribulation many will die from the comet and its tidal waves. All of the evil men will be dispatched from the earth by My purification of fire. I will bring My faithful to a safe place until the evil men are removed. Then, I will resurrect all of My faithful who will have died during the tribulation. This is the hope I give to all in this time, whether you survive this time or not. My faithful will receive glorified bodies, and return to a beautiful renewed earth that I will have prepared for you. This era of peace will last a thousand years as it was for Adam before the fall. Then, the Final judgement for all will come.*"

Later, at Nocturnal Adoration, I saw in space a wavering image of a diamond with various colors which represented some communication waves. Jesus said: *"My son, I come to you tonight, and I ask you to follow Me in every opportunity I send you, so you may spread My Word and My messages. Each thing that has happened in your mission, I have given you and I have presented all that is necessary to fulfill My will for you. When I asked My apostles to follow me, I did not ask for any excuses, but I asked for their full trust in leaving their wills behind. So it is with you, I am asking that whatever comes before you, that you treat these opportunities as moments of grace, to reach out in saving souls. Whenever you say 'yes' to My Will, you are stepping out in faith and I will reward you for your work. Look to the Holy Spirit for help to speak out in My Name, and bring My messages to the people. Do not hold back anything, from the people, that is necessary for their preparation for the events to come. I love all of My people, and I am sending My messengers as beacons of hope to lead the people through these times.*"

Sunday, August 18, 1996:

After Communion, I could see in the skies several angels coming forward on clouds blowing trumpets to announce a warning. Then I saw one angel come from a distance and in his wake I could see tremendous flames of chastisement that covered the whole sky. All at once I saw a picture of thousands of faces of souls all close to one another crying out for help. Jesus said: *"My people, I am announcing to you, through My angels, that the time of purification draws near. The angel of destruction is being called forth. Evil in your world is overflowing My cup of wrath. I have brought fire down on Sodom and Gomorrah for less than what you are doing. Since you are not changing your lives, and you have shut Me out of your lives, My cleansing fire of purification becomes My only option. You are seeing the souls crying out to be saved but they are bound under the hand of the evil one. I call My messengers forward in this crucial battle for souls. Do all in your power to save souls, especially, the ones in your own family. I give you an urgency to this appeal, since you do not have a long time for these souls to come to Me. Now is the time to hear My plea to come to Me for forgiveness of your sins. The Angel of judgement is coming soon, and it will be too late if these souls do not listen now. Go, warn My people to repent and be quick about it, since their time for conversion is short."*

Later, I saw on the earth some huge flying locusts with stingers like scorpions. They were sent as one of the plagues that will torment all of those who have turned against God. The locusts will sting these people short of death for a long time. Jesus said: *"My people, you are seeing My justice carried out on those who have rejected Me and refused to obey My commands. I wish to show those souls, who have not been converted, what they will face in this tribulation. I ask all of mankind to come to Me out of love, since I have made you and have redeemed you with My Blood. You, also, can come to Me out of fear of My wrath and justice as well, but please come before it is too late. For those who will not give themselves over to Me, you will face a dreadful torture such that you will wish you had never been born. After these plagues, the unfaithful will suffer the purification by fire. This will be a taste of hell on earth for a short time. Then I will cast the evil spirits and these lost souls into the eternal fires of hell. You will see after time stops, that you will be in the eternal now. Those sent to hell will never escape, and they will have eternal torment from the flames and from the anger of the demons who hate man. So, My friends, you should realize what you are choosing, when you make your life's decision. Will you choose the delight of the body in this world, which will send you to eternal punishment with no peace; or will you choose to love Me or come out of fear, and you will see My paradise of love in My oneness and eternal peace and rest for your souls? The choice is yours, but remember the consequences of your decision, and do not be deceived by the evil one or the pleasures of the body."*

Monday, August 19, 1996:

After Communion, I could see a platform as for where candidates for election would debate. Jesus said: *"My people, as your presidential elections get under way, these candidates appeal to the base instincts. Money and taxes are made the issue, instead of the moral decay of your country. The hard decisions on abortion, euthanasia, and drugs are the issues these politicians shy away from for fear of offending someone's likes or dislikes. It is because your people do not want to be disturbed in their sin, that many chastisements are befalling you. It is time your morality should be improved instead of ignored. If your politicians fail to take hard stands in bringing your country back to God, then they will reap the punishment due for your sins. Work to help your neighbor in government, instead of encouraging greed and more sin."*

Later, I could see a man with green and white markings on his shirt sleeve. He was giving out rations of grain to the people. Jesus said: *"Listen to Me, My people. I wish to stress this message to you tonight and follow Me. There is coming a great famine over all the earth. This will be one of the many coming chastisements to purify the earth. I have told you of such famines before as with Joseph and the Pharaoh's dream.* (Genesis 41:24-36) *Those who do not heed My Words, will suffer the ravages of starvation. At this time tell everyone and your government to make preparation for this trial. Put aside food and water for yourselves. It would be better that all peoples prepare as such, so that looting and stealing of food will not be rampant. I will be repeating this theme of, 'a ration of food will be given at the proper time.' This ration will be needed twice. First, before the tribulation, and then during the tribulation when I will provide My Manna for you in hiding. I am watching over you by giving you these warnings. These food shortages will later fall into the hands of the Antichrist, who will demand allegiance and his mark to buy and sell this food in short supply. It is at that time you must flee into hiding with My angel. He will show each of you your way, and provide you with the heavenly bread. Listen and heed My words, for your chastisements will be increasing."*

Tuesday, August 20, 1996:

Atfter Communion, I could see straight ahead that there was a burial place in the rock. Jesus said: *"My dear people, do not let your pride swell up in you, that you are better than any other man. As you see in this vision, that one day all of you must die. Never forget the body's mortality. This life is passing away quickly, so do not think much of what you possess or how smart you are, for these things will soon be taken from you. Instead, put your faith and trust in Me and concern yourself only with your soul's destination. I have shown you many times in scripture, that this life is only a testing area, where you can prove your faithfulness to My Word. Even in this decision, I give each of you the grace of faith through My ransom of the Cross. I love you My people, and I hold the door open to Heaven for all who choose to come. By showing your love for Me, and your love of neighbor, this will become your means to eternal salvation. Cast aside your own will and follow My Will, and you will find eternal glory with Me."*

Later, I saw Egyptian markings on a wall. I then travelled through some hallways to a large auditorium with empty seats and an empty stage. Jesus said: *"My people, I am showing you how the Antichrist will control the people who have the mark of the beast. He will call a meeting, and those with the chip will be summoned and controlled to listen to his suggestions and his brainwashing. It is important to realize that the Antichrist will not be able to find you if you do not take this chip. I have stressed many times not to take this chip, since then you will come under Satan's control. If you wish to be saved, you must trust in Me and reject the chip, even if it means death or torture. Believe in My words of hope and protection, for I will be your only alternative to Satan. I love you, My people, but you must pray for the strength to reject the world and place your full trust in My protection. Listen to My words and I will save your souls. All those who are saved, will see heaven on earth after the tribulation."*

Wednesday, August 21, 1996:

After Communion, I could see Jesus standing in heaven with open arms and with ethereal clouds all around Him. There was a brilliant light sending out peace and love all around Him also. Jesus said: *"My people, come to Me who shepherds His people with pure love itself. I am the object of all love, whether men want to believe it or not. I am the goal of your soul's desires. Earthly desires are a test, but I am the only one who will satisfy your soul's thirst for the divine. All souls by nature seek Me. It is only that you are imperfect by Adam's sin, that you do not fully comprehend Me. When you come to Me with glorified bodies, you will see My love and peace is all you could desire. Pray now that this veil of the world's ways may be lifted from you as blinders. Then you will truly see Me as I am, waiting to receive each soul into My Kingdom of Heaven. Give thanks to Me for all I have given you. I have given you Myself in dying for you on the Cross. If you believe in My love, then you must give your will over to Me, so you can be a part of My oneness."*

Later, at the prayer, group, I could see a small flame burning low and then it finally was snuffed out. I then saw a new candle replace the old one and the flame burned brightly again. Jesus said: *"My people, as time goes on in this evil age, many hearts grow weary and their faith in Me is snuffed out by the cares of the world. You are seeing a new flame of faith come, representing My warning, which will show all those fallen away how to return to Me. Awaken My souls who have lost their faith. Now will be the time of your enlightenment in My love."* I saw in a living room many objects and they all took on the color yellow. Jesus said: *"My people, remember the servicemen who were captured, and you remembered them with yellow ribbons. As the tribulation draws near, you will see more captives placed in your detention centers in your country. Now, you will see again religious and political persecution for all who object to the evil authorities."* I could see some cameras observing people as you see in the banks. Then, I saw chips located on the walls that could spy without people knowing they were watched. Again, I saw chips in the cable boxes that could see and listen as well. Jesus said: *"My people, I have shown you before how the evil men will use their devious electronic devices to watch your every move and even listen to your conversations. Be watchful, My people, that you may soon have to take out all of your electrical communications, so you will not be spied on. Listen to these warnings, since the evil ones will use your speech to show that you practice a religion outlawed by the state."* I could see the square at the Vatican and there was a spiraling action where all the people were cleared out of the square. Jesus said: *"Pray for the Holy Father, for he will have to suffer much at the hands of those trying to remove him from Rome. He will have to flee one day as you will flee from your persecutors. My Remnant Church will have to go underground to avoid the evil ones and practice your faith with your Rosaries as your weapon."* I could see a glimpse of Mary's face and there was a great light that shown all about her. Mary said: *"My dear children, I come with the light of my Son to light your way in faith. All who take my scapular and rosary with them, I will shield with my mantle of protection. No matter how much you are tested, if you stay true to my devotions, I will see you through these times. My Son's love of me and his faithful will never cease. As he protects the birds of the air, He will protect your souls even more so, since you are more valuable in your likeness to Him."* I could see a mother holding her newborn child close to her. Jesus said: *"My people, as you constantly say your prayers, I am constantly reminding you of the importance and sanctity of human life. You are all made in My image and you are all equal before My eyes. I see the unborn child just as important to have life as any one else in your society. See the hand of Satan behind your abortions, and struggle in prayer and action to fight this most vicious sin in your midst."* I could see a young child and a small constant flame held in front of him. Jesus said: *"My people, look to your young children that you instill the flame of faith in them by your example. Do not let any of My little ones wander in your bringing them up. See they are brought to Mass on Sunday no matter what their age. Teach them the sacraments especially, the forgiveness of sin in confession and the reception of Me in My Eucharist at the proper age."*

Thursday, August 22, 1996: (Queenship of Mary)
After Communion, I could see a glimpse of Maria E. and there was a large crowd that came up to a fence, but the altar area was bare. I then saw a picture in the sky of gold light and then Mary being given her crown. Mary said: *"My being proclaims the greatness of my God. My dear children, I cannot express in words how much I love my Son. He has made me blessed and He has given me His part of history that I may share. For the grace of my 'yes' to the angel, He has seen fit to have me reign as Queen and Mother of His people. He has raised me higher than His Saints and an-*

gels. My Son and I are one as you all are being called to His oneness. Strive to love Jesus as much and as often as you can. Your time on earth is precious and short. Give back some of that time to your Savior who will see your prayer and reward you fully. Continue in your struggle with me to save souls for my Son. Give glory and praise to God for all He has given you."

Friday, August 23, 1996: (Ezechial: Dead Man's Bones)
After Communion, I could see the old walled city of Jerusalem and the Via Dolorosa where Jesus carried His Cross. Jesus said: *"My people, you have seen in the readings, how I brought My people, Israel, out of captivity from the Babylonians. What you are seeing in the vision is where I brought all of My people out of the captivity of their sins. You have been fortunate to walk in My footsteps to Calvary. Now, all of you must make this trip to Calvary with your own crosses. If you love Me and appreciate My dying on the Cross for you, you will show your love by suffering your own cross on earth in following My Will. Put yourself in My hands and trust in Me, that I will lead you through life to your eternal destination with Me in Heaven. You only need follow Me these few years to show Me your love in life. Live out that love for Me every day of your life by offering all you do up to Me. Help Me daily also, when you help your neighbor."*

Saturday, August 24, 1996:
At St. Anastasia's Church, Troy, Michigan, after Communion, I could see two swords crossed. Jesus said: *"My people, I remind you of when Peter slashed the ear of one of the servants of those who arrested Me in the garden. I rebuked him by saying that those who live by the sword, will die by the sword. Those who would spread My message of love cannot take up arms in anger. This is the same message I give My followers during the tribulation. You must avoid wars and their consequences and live My Word of love even if it means death. You must flee the evil ones and leave behind the possessions that you do not need. I will provide the spiritual protection you will need. I will help you in the battle of good and evil, but not with man's weapons. I will use heavenly weapons as the Rosary and My Blessed Sacrament. I love all of you and you*

must place your trust in Me, so I can help you follow Me."

Sunday, August 25, 1996:

At St. Anastasia's Church, Troy, Michigan, after Communion I could see a mound of dirt as it was circling around. I looked up in the sky from the mound and I saw a huge angel the size of a 10 story building. Up above the angel there was a large white cross. The whole vision was awesome in this display of power. Jesus said: *"My people, you are witnessing in this vision the glory of My coming protection during the tribulation. You will see My angels visible in power before you at these places of refuge. The power and grace of My Presence will lead you to these safe havens. You will receive My Heavenly Manna from My angels. My angels will protect you from any evil spirits at that time. There will be such a glorious display of My grace and power at these permanent signs of My cross, that the faithful will flock to these places. You will see by these manifestations that I will not leave you orphans. My saving power will be among you in a miraculous way, that Satan will have no power over it. I have told you that fear is useless. Trust in My protection and I will see to all of your physical and spiritual needs."*

Later, I could see a poor house with some old vases and there were poor people walking around. Jesus said: *"My people, be careful when you talk about the poor, that you do not belittle them. Many of them will be walking to Heaven ahead of those who consider themselves well off, for My little ones have suffered want in this life, as the beggar Lazarus. Because they have suffered here already for their sins, it will go well with them in the next life. Those who have had money in this life could be enslaved by it. You have had everything you needed and have had little to suffer. Because of your love of money over Me and your little suffering, it will be very hard for the rich to be saved. Now you will truly understand why the first in this world, may be the last in the next world. Worship Me first, before any other thing in this world, and you will be on the road to Heaven. This is also why I have told you to give your money to the poor, if you wish to store treasures in Heaven, and show compassion on My less fortunate. Use your wealth for good, by sharing it, instead of for evil by being selfish with it."*

Monday, August 26, 1996:

After Communion, I could see some models of plane wings and a picture of the floor of the ocean signifying the TWA 800 flight. Jesus said: *"My people, has your world gone mad? Every day that you pick up the paper, you see senseless killings out of anger or in thievery. This latest downing, of the 230 people in terrorism, is even more senseless in the killing of innocent lives. Where is your society's death culture leading you? When you think nothing of killing defenseless little babies, is it any wonder that life is of little value to some? I tell you to stand up for your God given values in life, and defend life's preciousness or you will all be next at the hangman's hand. Life is too precious to be taken in anger or for any other reason. I am the giver and taker of life. Anyone, trying to act in My place by taking life, faces eternal death in the Fires of Gehenna. Watch and pray, My people, that you come to your senses and stop this wanton killing."*

Later, I saw an orchard and the ground was parched like a desert and the crops had withered away for lack of rain. Jesus said: *"My son, I have given you serious messages about the coming famine in your land. Do not waste time, but write to your government to notify the authorities to make preparation for this time. At first, men will deny there is such a threat. As time goes on, they will see and understand these things happening before their eyes. Go, therefore, and be quick to notify everyone that indeed a famine will strike over the whole world. To prepare properly, you must start even now to store food and water. You may not have much longer to decide to do something. Ask people to take action now or the food you want may not be there to store. I am blessing you all with this information. See to it that you put it to good use in helping others. If necessary, join together in groups to help store and buy food and water. This will be a further test of your trust in My words. You have seen many confirmations to know the truth of My words. Now you must carry out your duty to warn the people."*

Tuesday, August 27, 1996:

After Communion, I could see a large circular stone over a tomb in the rock. Jesus said: *"My people, I am the life and the resurrection. I am Lord over life and death. I am King of the*

Universe and Ruler over all peoples. See the power I have to raise the dead to life in today's reading. At My Second Coming, I will raise all the dead to life as they will be brought to judgement. Pray to Me and show Me how much you love Me, so at the judgement I will know you and welcome you into My banquet. Those, who refuse to accept me, will be sent to the everlasting fires of hell. I am advising all of My people not to judge anyone or violate another's life by killing in any way. You will be held accountable for anyone's blood on your hands. For I am the author of life, and I am the only one to call people to their home. Those, who take such life on their own, demand recompense for this greatest of sins."

Later, I could see it was night, and there were flaming bodies walking around that lit up the night giving it a reddish glow. Jesus said: *"My people, you are seeing how the evil men will be walking about at the end of the tribulation. They will be like the living coals of souls you saw in hell. My mercy and love reaches out to all My people, but many will not accept Me or My words. Some people have blocked everything religious out of their lives, since they do not want to give up their sinful lives. They do not want to be forced to do something against their will. Sooner or later the irony for these poor blind souls is that their suffering will become worse and never change. Pray for these lost souls that your prayers will make them open to My grace. If they are not awakened spiritually and come to Me for help, then they will be lost forever in the depths of hell. Come to Me, My people, before it is too late to be saved."*

Wednesday, August 28, 1996: (Feast of St. Augustine)

After Communion, I could see a priest with his back to me and he was approaching the Blessed Sacrament in the tabernacle. Jesus said: *"My people, I ask you to give Me thanks and praise for the priests that I send among you. Be thankful, especially, for the priests who bring you My Presence in the Eucharist at your daily Mass. Each priest is special to Me and should be to you also, since they represent Me on earth and lead My faithful to Me. They are the ones appointed to bring My sacraments and forgive sins through My power. Pray for your priests that they may re-*

main faithful to Me through attention to their prayer lives. Keep My priests close to your hearts and help them in their ministry in every way you can. Love My priests and every day give glory and praise to Me how you are blessed to have them. I have instituted My priesthood that My children may be led to Me and their gift of faith may be nourished. Cherish My priests and give them the respect of their office."

Later, at the prayer group, I could see a large single flame from a candle. Jesus said: *"My friends, look to the flame as a sign of My eternal love for My people. For those who pray to Me, I will take all of you under My hand of protection. Believe that at any time, even during the tribulation, you will never be tested beyond your endurance. Have faith and trust in Me that I will show you the way to your shelter. I will help provide you with all of your spiritual and bodily needs."* I could see many leaders of armies coming together to sign peace treaties. Jesus said: *"My people, many talk of peace and even go through the motions of signing peace treaties. Peace cannot be found in their hearts, since their pride will drive them to save face and wars will continue to break out. Unless you pray for My peace, man's peace will be fleeting. I repeat, as in the Scriptures, when they shout, 'peace, peace,' then will come sudden destruction. Continue to pray that peace will come over the land and touch the cold hearts."* I could see a drum being beaten. Jesus said: *"My people, many of your leaders say one thing, but later they are found doing something different. You will see as time goes on that many leaders in government and leaders connected to the bankers, are walking with a different drummer. They have a world agenda much different from representing their people. Instead, they are searching for fame and power without regard who they hurt. See these hypocrites for what they are and avoid them."* I could see some public spigots for water and other food being shut off. Jesus said: *"My people, in the future you will see that even water will be hard to come by. As food shortages appear and welfare is cut back, many people will find it difficult to find and buy food necessities. In your land of plenty you will see many blessings of good growing conditions will be taken away from you. See this as a sign of your sins which are weighing heavily against you. If you pray more and stop your abortions, then these chastisements will be lessened."* I could see the jaws of a large dragon open as he devoured many unsuspecting souls. Jesus said: *"My people, do not let Satan cloud your mind with all the desires and cares of this world. If you let your bodily desires go unrestrained and your prayer life weakens, you will be susceptible to the evil one leading you astray. You must stay on the narrow road in following My Commandments or you will fall down the wide road to losing your soul. Rid your selfishness in order to see My light."* I could see a door to a kitchen and it was being opened to let Jesus in. Mary came and said: *"My dear children, as my month of the Rosary comes, look to the power of the family Rosary to bring peace and love to your households. Open the door to my Son by offering your prayers together, so you can welcome my Son into your hearts. When a family is united in prayer, that house will be protected by my mantle and I will shelter you from outside or interior troubles."* I could see some old blackboards and baby cribs discarded in part of a junkyard. Jesus said: *"My people, I am showing you this scene because the little babies, that you are killing, will never get to use these cribs or experience going to school. See the importance of stopping these abortions, so these lives I have given a plan, may come to fulfillment. Do not thwart the life I have given, but avoid this sin of abortion. Pray for these mothers, that they will relent from killing their babies. Show them the true value of life by your evangelization."*

Thursday, August 29, 1996: (Beheading of John the Baptist)
After Communion, I could see an alarm clock and it was almost 12:00 midnight. Jesus said: *"My people, your time is running out before the start of the tribulation. Before all the great events in history, I have called forth my prophets and messengers to prepare the people and seek their conversion. Many of My prophets were killed because the messages were harsh and those evil people wanted to continue in their sin. But I would hear none of their rejection then, as I will hear none of it now. My words go forth by My messengers, so that you can come to Me before it is too late. Do not make the same mistake as those evil people in the past. The people of Sodom and Gomorrah continued sinning even until My purifying fire consumed them. For those who reject Me at this time, they will meet the same fate and worse, since many signs*

and messages will be given you. My warning will show you once and for all how your sins are seen by Me. So I tell you again, repent of your sins while you still have time for conversion. Escape the fires of My wrath by seeking My love and mercy. Those, who refuse Me, even with full knowledge of the consequences, are asking an even bitter avenging of My words of warning."

Friday, August 30, 1996: (Five Wise Virgins)
After Communion, I could see a woman gleaning the stubbles of the field for food. Jesus said: *"My people, you are now appreciating the true meaning of the word 'prepare' when I gave it to you for the title of your books. Now, in today's reading you can take advantage of seeing how all of you should be acting as the five wise virgins who secured oil for their lamps. They did this so they would be ready in waiting for the bridegroom. You have been graced with these warnings to prepare physically and even more importantly, spiritually for the time of famine and tribulation. It is unfortunate that there are still many foolish virgins who do not want to prepare, since they do not understand about future dangers. It is up to My wise virgins to tell all how to prepare. This is why I have asked you to get out these books by the fall. You all have succeeded in many of the tasks that I have requested, but your mission has just begun for a people with such hard hearts and deaf ears to My words. This stiff necked people have been acting as My people of Israel in past years. Do not be discouraged by many who will not listen, but pursue their souls as I do relentlessly. Food will be important for the coming famine, but do not let your physical instincts blind your faith in Me. It would be wise to keep My messages before the people as often as you can provide it. There will be an increasing urgency in the messages as they approach the time of tribulation. Heed My words of preparation, especially, the words of conversion in seeking My forgiveness of sins in confession. The soul, remember, is much more important than the body, so do not compromise My Commandments to take care of the body."*

Later, I could see some men with cowboy hats caring for their herds. Jesus said: *"My people, your farmers know better than you, just how severely their crops and animals have been treated this year. Many brush lands and woods are burning in the west with very little control over them by your firefighters. The farmers are having either droughts or flood waters to deal with in growing their crops. These farmers see My hand in these chastisements, and are seeing first hand the devastation of a good portion of their crops. See My hand is taking away the blessings I have given over your fertile fields. Blessings of good growing conditions are based on the people's faith in Me and how they follow My commandments. When a society rejects Me by ignoring My outstretched arms, then you are calling for My judgment. See that you pray much for families and sinners to come to Me in confession to have their sins forgiven. Until you ask for forgiveness, and admit you are sinners, how can you know Me and follow My Will? I love you, My people, and I come to each of you with My graces. Reach out and seek My help and I will lead you to the desire of your soul in heaven."*

Saturday, August 31, 1996: (Parable of the talents) After Communion, I saw an assembly line and people with different skills working. Jesus said: *"My people, as you see your labor day being celebrated, think of how I have endowed each person from birth with individual talents for their life's mission. This is why it behooves each person to discover their talents, and put them to the best use possible to fulfill your plan I have given each of you. If you become lazy and do not fulfill your use of My talents, you will have to account for such waste at the judgment as in the Gospel. Another waste of My gifts and talents is seen in your killing of the babies in abortion. These killed babies had certain talents that they were not permitted to carry out, and your society will not benefit from their skills as a result. Not only is it a loss to you, but it thwarts My plan for their lives in how they would have made their contributions to life. This sin of abortion, therefore, wears heavy on the judgment of each nation that permits abortion. See the many afflictions of problems and chastisements that are coming down on you as a result. Fight this evil with prayer and any of your talents that you can use to turn back this tide of sin."*

Later, I could see a man with some fruit and then a house on the beach. Next, I could see out into the ocean and it was very calm. Suddenly, I could see a large tidal wave engulf a small boat. An earthquake in the ocean had caused the wave. Jesus said: *"My people, you are again seeing another sign of the End Times in this vision. Earthquakes have been occurring with a higher frequency. They, also, will be increasing in intensity. There will be some severe earthquakes possibly in the Pacific Ocean which may cause some flooding in some areas. When you see these events occurring in rapid succession, as I have told you, you will realize your time of My purification draws near. Again, I tell you that many of these chastisements will fall on areas of greater sin. Hear My plea for prayers, so you can pray for peace and the conversion of sinners. Never lose sight even working to save those souls around you, especially in your own families."*

Sunday, September 1, 1996:

After Communion, I could see some crawling bugs and worms down in the ground. I could feel myself down in the ground with them. Jesus said: *"My people, when I came on the earth, I became a worm among men. I humbled Myself to become a man in the stable of Bethlehem. When I grew older, I had no home of My own. When I died for you on the Cross, men spat on Me and uttered all indignations at Me. You, my friends, will soon be treated in such a way for believing in My Name, as men grow more evil. Let My life be a lesson to you, not to seek fame and fortune in this passing life. Do not be seeking praise for your labors or your good works. Seek only to please Me and follow My commands in the Scriptures. Then you will be rewarded in the next life which lasts forever. Seek Me and the life that endures, not this world which will be thrown on the fire and consumed in a short time. I love you, My people, and I want you to act humbly in this life, seeking the lowly instead of the lofty. Then you will give example to others of My humility."*

Later, I could see some harvest machines on the side and another machine turning over the earth. Instead of harvesting crops, only the dirt with hay could be returned. Jesus said: *"My people, I will tell you now, that one of the fall events that I have warned you about, deals with the extent of crop damage and the huge losses farmers will have to bear. Again, the effects of this reduc-*

tion in crops will affect your food prices and cause gyrations in your agricultural markets and your stock markets. I have mentioned to you about the coming world famine. As the weather affects your harvests, many will begin to see that My words are to be reckoned with. You have been given many warnings about food shortages. When these things happen around you, many troubles will occur in your cities as people look to secure food for themselves. Your grocery markets will find it harder to keep their shelves stocked as panic will cause buyouts and hoarding. These happenings will bring the time of tribulation ripe for the Antichrist to come on the scene. It is such a chaos of problems that people will be drawn to him to solve. In all of these trials look to Me as your light of hope. Those, who stick by Me in faith, will win out in the end, as I will protect you from the evil ones."

Monday, September 2, 1996: (Labor Day)

After Communion, I could see many long narrow roads leading to a huge altar. Jesus said: *"My people, all roads lead to Me. Some may wonder at the meaning of these words. I have bequeathed each person with certain talents, so they may find work by their hands. As each person has different skills, their plan of life I have given them will lead them to their salvation, if they follow My Will. Some will deviate from these roads of life and find many problems as a result. Other roads that are followed will eventually lead to Me at the judgement. So, in the last analysis whether you follow My plan or not, you will have to make an accounting for your life. If you have used your talents properly and have followed My plan for you, I will welcome you into My Kingdom. Those, who have used their talents for their own gain, along the broad road to the abuses of My gifts, will face the grinding and gnashing of teeth as they are cast into the fiery furnace. The road you choose will determine your soul's fate. So remember, My love awaits everyone, but the end of each road must face me at the judgement."*

Later, I saw several scenes of bridges across rivers. Jesus said: *"My people, I am the bridge between your world and the next world which is blessed by My peace. Anyone, who seeks Heaven or salvation, must come through Me. It is I who have given you everything in your possession. Your most precious gift is to be able to receive Me in Holy Communion. It is then that you experience My Presence and My peace. In order to obtain Heaven, you must give yourself entirely over to My Will. It is only when you love Me and wish to do everything for Me, that you will see how I bridge the gap between the spiritual life and your physical life. I am divine and man at the same time. This is how I can provide the link between the Father and all of mankind. Come to Me, My people, and let Me lead you to Heaven, so you too, can know the purified body and glorified spirit you will have."*

Tuesday, September 3, 1996:

After Communion, I could see an aisle in a Church. I then could see a huge snake or dragon with dripping fangs lunging out at the people. Jesus said: *"My people, you are seeing how Satan is spreading his evil venom of sin, even through some of My clergy. For those misled by the evil one, there is a pride of giving their own theology, instead of the truth. These same priests are speaking out against My Pope son. This evil schism is building over time, since they do not want to be held in obedience to the teachings of the Church. This modernism and liberation theology is far from what I gave to My apostles and is misleading the faithful. Listen to My words through My Pope son, John Paul II, and he will lead you on the right path to your salvation. Test the spirit of whatever is preached, so you can discern My truths, and see if they are being taught properly. Do not be surprised when a schism in My Church will come, but follow My faithful remnant led by John Paul II."*

Later, I could see a long bench where judges sit. Jesus said: *"My people, could anyone gather enough evidence to prove that you are a Christian or not? It is one thing to hear My message of love and peace, but another to live My message every day following My Will. You will one day face your own judgment. If you have proclaimed My message as I have asked, you will fulfill your duty. But if you try to soften or excuse what I have said for a better hearing, then you will be badly mistaken. Do not be totally concerned with mellowing the messages so they are more acceptable. The true story has to be told, and what I have given you should be taken to heart. If people refuse to listen because they are too harsh, then pray for them to be more open. You cannot make excuses to continue living an easy life. It is important that people are taken out of their comfort zone. It is only through suffering, and the following of My Will, that you will gain your crown."*

Wednesday, September 4, 1996: (US 27 & 17 missiles in Iraq) After Communion, I could see some planes causing destruction and some of the planes were in flames. Jesus said: *"My people, why do you insist on carrying out your weapons of war against your neighbor? War making in any situation is not from Me, but comes from the anger in the hearts of men, and many times it is inspired by the evil one. I warn you in every situation not to widen any conflict by even more killing and destruction. War is a catalyst for perpetuating the unrest among peoples. Do not pray for man's peace, but pray that My peace will come over the hearts of these recent combatants. If the evil one can encourage you to kill one another, he is winning a battle in this struggle for souls. Come to your senses quickly, and do not let these incidents grow into a wider war that you may have no control over. If you fail to listen to My pleas, you may suffer the consequences at your own hands. Remember as I told you, those who live by the sword, will die by the sword."*
Later, at the prayer group, I could see a yellow plastic device which looked like some kind of a gun, but it was the device to implant the mark of the beast. Jesus said: *"My people, I am showing you how the mark of the beast will be implanted in people's right hand. This is the chip that I have told you to avoid at all costs, even if it will prevent you from buying food. Those who take the Mark knowingly, and are not forced, will be lost to Satan's control. I will provide you food, so do not take this device under any condition."* I could see blankets and bedding being provided at a school for those fleeing this latest storm, Fran. Jesus said: *"My people, you may see some major damage from this storm and the rest of this storm season. Pray that the people evacuate to avoid any loss of life. These chastisements are coming to take away some of your possessions. You have an abundance of things, but are many times lacking in spiritual possessions. See these earthly things are not to be praised, and only praise Me."* I could see armaments being loaded on some

U.S. planes. Jesus said: *"Be careful, My people of America. Your leaders may take you down a path to war where your sons' lives may again be placed on the line for the bankers who want their oil interests protected. This region is central to the world's oil, and this could become a prize other nations may seek to take for themselves. Pray for peace, because the motives of some of these leaders may be for their gain, without regard for human lives."* I could see Our Lady come and she was holding many rosaries. Mary said: *"My dear children, as you celebrate my feast day, I bring you my Rosary as your weapon against the evil of this age. Pray my Rosary often as you are tonight. Much prayer is needed to balance the sin being committed in your world. Unless more prayers are said for peace and the conversion of sinners, I will not be able to hold back my Son's justice. He has told you, the severity of your trials will lie in the balance of how much prayer is said. Therefore, double your efforts now to lessen these punishments."* I could see some scenes of people on the beach, but these pictures were upside down. I then saw many waves of water come rushing against the shore. Jesus said: *"My people, you will see events turned upside down in that there will be continuous events of disaster. Before one event is over, you will see the next happening in a short time. See these things happening as the tribulation comes, and the time is shortened for the sake of the elect."* I could see a vast expanse of ruins of an old civilization. All of the buildings had been destroyed. There was nothing left standing but the footings and basements of these dwellings. Jesus said: *"My people, heed this vision of past civilizations. Many have arisen, but they all have come to ruin. Most of these civilizations collapsed from within from immorality and their greed. I have many times allowed this destruction of these societies, since they rejected Me and committed all manner of abominations in My sight. Heed this warning, since your nation is headed down this path to destruction as well."* I could see a separation of darkness and a bright light. Jesus said: *"My people, you are called to my light as I curse the darkness. There is among you an ongoing battle between good and evil. This struggle you can see before your eyes, because it is a struggle to save souls. See this as an important battle, that you must fight for Me every day, in setting a good example to others. Keep focused on Me, and I will send you My graces to fight the evil ones, and work to save souls at this time."*

Thursday, September 5, 1996:

After Communion, I could see several friends and Carol receiving Holy Communion in a big auditorium as at some conference. Jesus said: *"My son, you indeed are seeing some future conferences. If you are willing to continue doing My Will of spreading My messages, I will provide the forum by which you can reach many souls. Continue your daily prayers and more with every waking hour. You will need strength to fight the evil one in your battle for souls. I will work miracles of conversion on those who read these books with an open mind. Continue in this publication as long as time and conditions permit. Do not be fearful of any adversity against My messages. I will find ways around your problems, so My truths will be made known. This is a critical time before the tribulation, and many souls need to be touched by My grace of opportunity, so they can be saved. Continue to listen to Me, My child, and continue following My Will."*

Friday, September 6, 1996:

After Communion, I could see some tall pillars of columns as in a courthouse. Jesus said: *"My people, you should take note of the readings today, so that you understand about the difference between man's justice and My justice. It is not your place to make judgments of others, but instead leave this to My Will. Man's justice is very limited in that you usually only perceive it from one vantage point — your own. It usually is quickly done without thinking of the consequences or full knowledge of the circumstances. Even though many make judgments, it is still not your place to do so. So avoid making judgments. You will not find true justice among men, so do not expect all of your dealings to be fair. Look to My justice and be satisfied that I will deal with all of the evil doers. Do not be consumed with your own righteousness, that you should receive better treatment than others. You would be more cautious, if your measure of justice was used by others against you. Accept My advice on this subject, and lavish love on each other, instead of judgments. It is sometimes these thoughts on making judgments that drive many to fighting and wars, where they feel they have been wronged. Live a life of love, thinking good of each other, and leave the judgments to Me alone."*

Later, I could see many views of Jesus dying on the cross. I could see Him willing to share His pain so the world could be saved. Jesus said: *"My people, realize that I died on the Cross once, but know that I died equally for each sinner who lives now, for those who will be, and for those who have died. Each of you is faced with life's decisions to either follow My ways or reject them. There can be no middle ground, for you are either with Me or against Me. My death on the Cross shows you how much I love all of you. Love is life, since it gives life purpose and encourages your love for Me. When hate controls your life, then death, both physically and spiritually, takes over. Look to Me for love and My peace which*

encourages harmony among all men. When the love of two people becomes self-giving, then new life is generated by their offspring. When man is united to God in love, the two become as one. When you understand divine love by My example in marriage, you start to appreciate My reason for creating you, so I can share that love. By uniting yourself with Me in prayer, you can see how you must share your love with Me and your neighbor as well."

Saturday, September 7, 1996:

After Communion, I could see Our Lady and her head was bowed down for her birthday. Mary said: *"My dear children, I wish to come and share my feast day with you. Come, join in your Rosary groups to storm heaven with your prayers for my intentions. I love you, my children, and as a mother, I love to give you the comfort of my Son. Every time I come, I bring you my Son as well. You are seeing many events take place and many with loss of life. Pray for these souls who are dying and for those who need conversion. My Son has asked you to be always vigilant with prayer, since you know not when you will be brought before the judgment at your own death. Life is very fragile in your state now, so treasure every moment that you can give everything over to my Son's Will."*

Later, I could see the Host exposed for adoration. Suddenly, I could see the vision cut in two, right through the Host. Jesus said: *"My people, you are seeing in this vision, how the demons will inspire people to hate Me in the presence of My Blessed Sacrament. The demons know the power of Holy Communion, and*

they will get the people to desecrate My Hosts, and teach that My Presence is not there. These evil people will even seek the Hosts for black masses. At that time when My tabernacles are in danger of desecration, My faithful will have to protect and guard these hosts from destruction. You will have to keep My Hosts in hiding to preserve the sacredness of My Presence. While you can worship Me in My Blessed Sacrament, take advantage of My graces present there. Soon, you may not have this convenience much longer. Men will then hate those who are religious. When the persecution begins, you will see the evil men strike at My Hosts. This, again, will be a sign of the tribulation among you. Praise Me in My Real Presence, and thank Me for My gift of the Eucharist to all of mankind."

Sunday September 8, 1996: (Our Lady's Birthday)

After Communion, I saw a huge crowd with a palm tree on one side and an image of the grim reaper on the other side. I then saw another crowd from ground level and a man was wearing a sombrero. Finally, I saw up from a distance there were some huge floods overrunning the land. Jesus said: *"My people, you are seeing people in panic for their lives. As these storms continue, you will see many mass evacuations and much ensuing damage. When they return to their damaged houses, many will be displaced from their jobs and their possessions will be ravaged. Food will be expensive and scarce, especially, in these damaged areas. By your vision you are seeing this happen in more southern area. At first, people will be anxious to start over. Then, as these storms become more frequent, many hardships will cause many financial problems. If you do not realize that these chastisements are a punishment for your sins, you will be brought to your knees out of desperation for help. Pray, My people, that you may come to your senses and praise Me instead of your possessions."*

Later, at Jack Shea's house, I could see Our Lady walking on the ground among us in vision. She was crying tears of sorrow. Mary said: *"I am happy to walk among you this evening. Thank you for coming to say my Rosary, even with the rainy weather. Many of you know that this is my weather at all of my shrines. I wish to direct your prayers to stopping abortion in your country.*

My tears are flowing now and the statues are weeping for the killing of these babies. My Son is very displeased with this disregard for life as well. Many of your chastisements have been coming for this, more than any other sin. You have leaders in this fight against abortion. I am asking your prayers and your public witness against these sins of abortion. Both prayer and action are most powerful in this battle. If you do not speak out against this evil, you will be held responsible for the results of your inaction. When God's laws are violated so blatantly, it is your duty to instruct your brothers and sisters of their errors."

Monday, September 9, 1996:

After Communion, I could see a lady's face but she was veiled behind some dark grey shades as if under the control of the evil forces. Jesus said: *"My son, there are many of My children asleep in their sin, waiting to be brought to Me. I am calling on you to go forth and awaken their spirits to My call for conversion. My message needs to be taken to the people, even where you may encounter resistance to the message. By bringing your books and My messages before the people, My graces will go forth to raise this veil of evil blindness. Pray over the people, so they can be released from their chains of both physical and spiritual problems. Instill in people a faith and hope in Me, which is necessary for them to be saved. Never fear any adversity, but bring My peace and love to all who wish to hear My message. This age of evil has its days numbered, but it will not give up without a fight."*

(Note: After talk at Corpus Christi) Later, I could see a column of army vehicles moving forward. Jesus said: *"My son, you are seeing in this vision how I send My messengers into battle against the evil of this world. Go forth and preach My Gospel message with faith and courage in Me to help you. My messages reach out to their hearts and speak to them of conversion. My love beckons all of My people to seek forgiveness of their sins. Your work in the harvest of souls is much needed. So keep faithful to your calling and keep reaching out for souls in this time when preparation is most needed. Ask My grace and the Holy Spirit to continually support you in speaking to the people. You do not realize how much My faithful are seeking the sacred and true rest for their souls. Your praying with the people is another outpouring of My love, which you should continue to share with those in need. Give praise and thanks for My gifts and spread them with abundance to all who will listen and accept My words."*

Tuesday, September 10, 1996:

After Communion, I could look around an ancient wall and I saw Jesus suffering on the cross and there was darkness all over. Jesus said: *"My people, you are seeing Me as I suffered for you on the Cross. Look on this as an example for your own lives. When you come to Me and give your will over to Me, life will not be easy, and you will be asked to suffer for My sake. Suffering and giving up an easy living is the best way to purify your souls. Take advantage of this testing time to prove your love for Me, despite dificulties that may come up. You will see My reward for your faithfulness will far surpass anything you are asked to suffer for Me. See the beauty of My peace and love come over your life as you serve Me here. Service in the Gospel message is what every servant is called to do from the roots of your baptism. Live your faith by following My will in your daily ministry."*

Later, I could see a lighted and housed container which held some precious stones. Jesus said: *"My people, if I were to ask each of you what is most precious to you here on earth, how would you respond? Some may answer, one of their loved ones or one of their possessions. Some of faith may answer God or their faith. When I look on each of you, I see your soul and this alone is precious to Me, even if you are a great sinner. I look on your tears of love as special also, since I know what you are expressing comes sincerely from the heart. See that those things that are eternal and everlasting, are those things or beings that should be most important to you. Your soul is immortal and therefore will live forever. That is why your soul is most precious to Me, and also it should be for you. Once you have committed your life to Me, you will see that other souls are just as important to me. That is why saving souls for Me is the best gift you can bring to Me. Whatever you can do to lead souls to Heaven should be your first priority in life. It is the beauty of this understanding of life that makes everything clear in your eyes, to know the mission in life I ask of all of My faithful. 'Go out to all the nations and preach the Good News of Salvation.' "*

Wednesday, September 11, 1996:

At the Blessed Sacrament Church, Charleston, S.C., I could see a tall yellow loudspeaker which was used by the Antichrist to direct the people. Jesus said: *"My people, you are seeing during the tribulation how the Antichrist will rule over the people. Many will have their movements watched, and speakers will be all around to direct them to worship him. Worshipping the Antichrist will seem a small price to have food and jobs given to them. The price of belonging to the world will be your soul. Those who follow Me, will be tortured and suffer humiliation for My sake. Those who give in to the world, will seem to have everything for a while, but they will suffer greatly later. Do not be deceived by the miracles and pleasures offered by this evil one, for the wages of sin is death to the soul. See the real folly will be to follow the world. Following Me may seem a harder road to endure, but the reward will be joy with Me in Heaven and on earth. Remember to follow Me wherever I will lead you, and I will show you to My Father. Have faith and trust in Me and all My gifts to you will be more than you can imagine."*

Thursday, September 12, 1996:

At the Blessed Sacrament Church, Charleston, S.C., I could see an altar with some chairs on it and it was dark. I then was led to the side and down a dark road away from that church. Jesus said: *"My people, you are seeing a church during the tribulation, as it was being used only to worship the Antichrist. At that time the evil people of that age will be living in their sin, and receiving their food and jobs through the Antichrist's agents. These lost souls will be content only for worldly desires, and will not even care about Me. Their only concern will be to follow those evil authorities to get what they want. My faithful, who desire to worship Me only, will have to suffer as outlaws in hiding. Those faithful, who defy these evil rulers, should follow Me and your angels to My places of protection. Otherwise, you will be sent to prisons or detention centers, where you will be tortured and some martyred. At My refuges, I will provide food and protection from the evil men. Trust in Me at that time, so I may lead you through the desert of evil to a land of milk and honey, after the evil one's reign. In a short time, I will settle accounts with all of you at the first judgement of the age of tribulation. My Final Chastisement will deal a lethal blow to all evil on the earth. I will then take you up, and renew the earth, as I ready you for My era of peace. Keep faith and hope in Me at all times, and I will lead you to your salvation, despite all of these heavy trials. Remember, I will always be at your side to guard you from the evil ones."*

Later, at adoration in Blessed Sacrament Church, Charleston, S.C., I could see some houses or displays with a carnival and a large ferris wheel. Jesus said: *"My people, many people are only interested in the powerful and unusual messages. In addition, some want to hear only the most recent of messages, so they can be up to date. You must realize, My people, that I am not giving you messages, as you are used to on your daily news. Instead, I give you those things which you need to know for the moment and no more. Do not look for explicit dates. My real messengers rarely give dates. My message has been the same for many years, and it all comes down to you giving your will over to Me. Many are so taken in by the pleasures and cares of the world, that they want control of what to enjoy in life. I have asked for suffering, also, but many are too comfortable to want to give up their easy life. I tell you, My people, if you really love Me and want to attain salvation, you must give up the pleasures of this world, so you can purify your souls. When you live to help Me by helping others and thinking less of yourselves, only then will you be able to profit from your testing on earth. Suffer in constant prayer and fasting for My intentions. Donate as much money as you can for the poor, since you cannot be selfish. Learn to appreciate all the messages, even the older ones, so you may complete your perfection in knowing My Will."*

Friday, September 13, 1996:

At Blessed Sacrament Church, Charleston, S.C., I could see the pews of a large church. Jesus said: *"My people, you have your roots in the church I have entrusted to My apostles. Through the years My faithful have had to endure many hardships, but in the end My church has survived. I have told you that My Church would last to the end of time. Even in your very time, you have enjoyed the ability to worship Me without harassment. In your country, you have enjoyed a religious freedom won for you by your predecessors. This is why suffering for the Gospel is an unusual request to a people that have had their freedom from persecution for a long time. Yet, I tell you, you will soon have to suffer for My Name's sake, if you would remain a true disciple of mine. As this evil age reaches its height of reign, you will see much persecution. The evil people of this age want to do what they will, instead of obeying My commands. All men will undergo a time of apostasy when the Antichrist will demand worship only be given to him. In this tribulation I will have My angels protect you. They will lead you to safe havens away from these evil men. Be faithful to Me, even more so in these coming years, and I will be your rock of salvation, despite the worst Satan will try. Pray for My help to console you, and I will lead you to a wonderful heaven on earth."*

Later, at the Blessed Sacrament Church, Charleston, S.C., I could see a man trapped in a web, and behind him everything was aglow in red. Jesus said: *"My dear people, it is important that you be prepared to know the powers and plans of the Antichrist. He will be the most evil man to come to the earth. He will have miraculous powers, since he will be like a devil incarnate. He must be avoided at all costs, because of his hypnotic power over people, and his charisma to attract followers. His evil will be very subtle at first, as he plays the part of a peacemaker. He will be very clever and a father of lies. People will believe his promises and will be drawn into his web of evil. He will seek out souls by buying them with this world's goods, if they would only worship him. Avoid all electrical communications, since he will have power over the people on TV and the internet. Because I have warned you beforehand, realize My words are true, and when you see them fulfilled, do follow Me for safety. I will protect you from all evil, if you pray for My help. My safe havens will assure you of protection from the evil spirits at all times. Choose My way over the Antichrist, since I offer you eternal life, but he can only offer eternal death and suffering. Come to My loving heart, My people, and I will give you the peace and rest that your soul has sought from the beginning."*

Saturday, September 14, 1996:

At St. Therese Church, Mooresville, N.C., after Communion, I could see Jesus seated on a throne of judgment. Jesus said: *"My people, I am seeking you every day that you may be converted from your worldly will to following My Will. The readings speak of forgiveness, and I offer you My death on the Cross in payment of your sins. I have instituted the Sacrament of Reconciliation for you to confess your sins to Me through the priest. In order to be saved, you must first recognize yourself as a sinner. All men are weak and sinners as a result of Adam's fall. If you do not admit to being a sinner, then you are denying the reality of your place in life. Come, My children, I welcome each of you to My forgiveness, if you would only come with contrite hearts seeking My mercy. Those, who do not seek My mercy in Confession, will be told at the judgement how I do not know them and they will be accursed. All those, who seek My forgiveness, are seeing a model in Me. I am willing to forgive unconditionally, without limit for the number of times you request My forgiveness. If you would be My disciple, I ask you to treat your brothers and sisters in like fashion. That is, forgive your neighbor for whatever wrong he has committed, and forgive him as often as he seeks forgiveness from you. In seeking My forgiveness, and forgiving your neighbor, you will be directed closer in your perfection. For this service, I will acknowledge you before men and before My Father, and you will be welcomed to your eternal reward."*

Sunday, September 15, 1996:

At Blessed Sacrament Church, Charleston, S.C., after Communion, I could see a very tall white building. This represented how far away the Lord puts away the sight of our sins. Jesus said: *"My people, in the Gospel I told My apostles to forgive seventy times seven times. I ask each of you to think of how many sins you have committed in your whole life, even including all of your venial sins. Then, think how I have forgiven all of them, when you were sorry and requested My forgiveness of your debt. My mercy for each of you is everlasting. He that repents of his sins, I will always forgive, I cannot deny the promise I give even to the most grievous of sinners. I love all of you, and I wish to erase all sin that comes between us. Sin is the only impediment in the way of your love being perfected. When you can use My help through prayer and fasting to avoid sin as much as you can, you are coming closer to My reign. I have asked you also, to make amends with your brother before you bring your gift of love to My altar. If you would love Me, you must love and forgive your brother as well. Seek to understand My mercy as much as possible, so you will see to it in your heart to grant mercy on others. See My life and My words are a model of living for you in pleasing My Father. When you settle accounts, you will see how much you have followed My Will and My ways. I know of your imperfections, so do not be afraid to seek My forgiveness in Confession. I have given my love to the utmost of My being for all of mankind when I gave up my life for you and your sins."*

Monday, September 16, 1996:

At Blessed Sacrament Church, Charleston, S.C., after Communion, I could see an altar, and behind it was a beautiful white light. The Host was being lifted up at the Consecration. Jesus said: *"My people, I am the Light of the World as you see this white light behind the altar. I am the gift of life for all of mankind. I have given My life up for you, that all of you may have life within you. I speak not just of the physical life I create in you, but I bring a spiritual life to you, which refreshes your soul with a living water. I make Myself available to you in My Bread from Heaven in the Consecrated Host by My priest. I have given you My Sacrament of the Eucharist to have My Real Body and Blood in the bread and wine. This is a food of angels which I have gifted to you at the last supper. Be thankful, My friends, for this true gift of life which your soul is forever seeking. My love I pour out on you, and I beckon you to receive Me with a soul purified from all sin by confession. As the centurion said he was not worthy, you too must be properly ready to receive Me. My gift of Blessed Union awaits you at every Mass, but do not receive Me with mortal sin on your soul. Do not commit continuous sacrilege without first asking My forgiveness of your sins. Then, when you receive Me into a pure heart of love, I will come and envelop you with My graces. I will protect you from the evil one as well.*

There is great spiritual power in My Blessed Sacrament. Be thankful that I have visited My people in this way."

Later, at Blessed Sacrament Church, Charleston, S.C., I could see some animals and they were being lifted up higher. Jesus said: *"My people, you are witnessing the change in the animal kingdom during the era of peace. I have told you how man will be in harmony with Me and himself. You will be young again and perfectly formed, so you will not experience death or sickness. Eating to survive will not be necessary, so that you will be a vegetarian if you choose to eat. All the animals around you will be perfected, and young as you with no death nor sickness. Animals will not kill each other for food, since they also will not require food for survival. All on earth will be in harmony with My will, as it was before Adam's fall. You will see a beauty among nature that you cannot now fully appreciate. Every animal, down to the least insect, will be precious to Me, and you shall not destroy any of them. Instead, you will have full knowledge and understand why they must be as you are, existing free of any evil threats. When you live in My Divine Will, you will be experiencing the perfection that I desire of you on earth. See this life and the era of peace as a preparation for your entry into Heaven, to enjoy My presence in the eternal now. When you reach Heaven, you will fully understand how I have led you on your path, to experience the divine in all of its dimensions of love and peace. Live for the day to be with Me in Heaven, and start by giving over your will to Me in all you do."*

Tuesday, September 17, 1996: (St. Robert Bellarmine)

At Blessed Sacrament Church, Charleston, S.C., after Communion, I could see a long hall in a beautiful Church. Along the side there was a large white shroud that seemed draped over various holding spots. The last spot showed a drop in the shroud that was lower than the rest but still continued. Jesus said: *"My people, you are seeing by this shroud, a continuation in the reign of my popes. Now, with this last pope, you are seeing it lower, since you will see a time of persecution that will split My Church. My Pope John Paul II will lead My Remnant Church, but an impostor pope will mislead even some of My faithful. At the tribulation this evil pope will be in league with the Antichrist. Do not believe in what he says, but follow My sacred scriptures in its proper teachings. You all will be jolted out of your security, but My protection will be a prayer away. Come to Me, My children, in your trial and I will show you the way to safety. Depend on Me in full trust, and I will provide for all of your needs. Do not complain over these tests, for it will be through them that you will be given your crown of My glory. Keep faithful to Me in all of My requests, and I will reward you with a gift of love no one can take from you."*

Later, at Blessed Sacrament Church, Charleston, S.C., I could see some thick stone arches holding up a Church. Jesus said: *"My people, I have placed My Church in the hands of Peter, whom I called a Rock, and the Gates of hell shall not prevail against it. Mere men could not carry on My Church, but I have inspired these leaders through the power of the Holy Spirit. It is the power of My Holy Spirit, that even today keeps the faith vibrant in My Remnant Church. My true faithful love Me, despite their trials, and are committed with My help to preserve My Church. When My disciples love their friends and are at peace during good times, what merit is there in that? It is when you are tested by those who love you and your enemies, that you must persevere with love. It is when you are tested even with every day little trials, that you must remain calm. When you hold your anger in check in diffi-cult situations, that is when you gain the most merits for your restraint. Do not be upset with worldly discomforts, but suffer each day for Me in bearing your trials gracefully. Avoid those places of temptation for sin, and pray often to strengthen your resolve to do good. Live a life of love and show that love to Me and your neighbor. Help those around you in any way you can, so you will live My commands and follow the beatitudes."*

Wednesday, September 18, 1996:

After Communion, I could see a picture of a woman on a cloth dressed in elaborate make-up. Jesus said: *"My people, you are see-ing in this vision an image of how you have been taken up by the world. Many are thinking of themselves only in the way you dress, in the things you desire and in your actions of how you crave the things of this world. All things, that are natural, are good in them-*

selves. It is the things man has made that sometimes become a god to you. Man has become so selfish that many things he does are for his own satisfaction. Do not forget God or your neighbor in life. As in the reading, love is what binds you together with Me and others. If you cannot go outside of your own desires, you will never be able to have a knowledge of My love. Place Me first in your life and follow My Will, then all things will be given you besides. If you depend on yourself only, you will be caught in Satan's web of desiring only the things of this world. These things are gone tomorrow, so seek heavenly things through Me that will be everlasting. To love, you must give of yourself to Me and others without worrying about your own desires. When you do everything for Me and others out of love, then you will find Me present in all of mankind. Learn this lesson of love, because it is an eternal lesson you must know to be with Me."

Thursday, September 19, 1996:

After Communion, I could see Maria E. and she said: *"Join with Jesus in his Blessed Sacrament."* I then had a vision of a donkey. Jesus said: *"My people, there are many in your country, and outside of your country, that are concerned about your upcoming elections. You could see some drastic revelations forthcoming, that could alter the outcome of these elections. Your country lies on the brink of some serious decisions, as its moral decay is leading you to ruin. However your people vote, may determine eventually whether there will be a turn around in your spiritual thinking or not. Your government's actions ultimately will determine whether your chastisements will lessen or worsen. I do not threaten My people, but I am merciful and just. You are the ones by your actions that will determine your destiny. However the outcome, you must know that My purification is coming as evil reaches its reign. Pray, My children, and I will direct your actions."*

Later, at the prayer group in Church, I could see Jesus on the cross shining His light against the darkness of the night. Jesus said: *"My people, I am your beacon of light, love and peace. Look to Me as your strength against all the evil in this world. I give you hope through My very life offered up for you on My Cross. My Precious Blood is poured out on all of you in forgiveness of your sins. Seek Me when you desire freedom from your sins."* I could see a man wearing a turban and he was at the head of a circle of ten men. Jesus said: *"My people, I have asked you many times to prepare for the End Times, when the Antichrist will have his short reign. This will be a test for you, and a chance for you to listen and understand My words of preparation. Come to Me, My children, in faith, and I will protect you through this tribulation."* I could see some doctors and nurses in a hospital with masks over their faces. There were many suffering patients all over the floor. Jesus said: *"My people, during these days of purification, you will see many strange diseases afflict the people. Many will be stricken, and contagious diseases will spread among you like wildfire. See these tests again as trials in your tribulation. If you look on My Cross, or pray to your angels, these diseases will be cured."* I could see a women in black as Mother Cabrini and she said: *"My son, I am happy to see you are planning to come to the area of my shrine. Please stop and visit me, so I may help you in your mission. Thank these wonderful people, who have invited you here. I am watching over you because of your remembering me."* I could see a night scene and the moon had turned blood red with flames about. Jesus said: *"My people, look to the sky for the signs of My visitation. When you see the moon turn blood red, it will be a sign to you of the tribulation among you. Evil men will spread their hate among you, but My love will guard you against them. Have faith in My help even amidst the darkness of evil. This, also, will be a sign of the wars that will be all over the land."* I could see Mary come also as a light in the night. She was guiding the people back to Church and to her Son. Mary said: *"Thank you, my children, for coming closer to my Son, by your prayers before my Son's Blessed Sacrament. In all I do, asking for your prayers for peace and conversion, I bring you to Jesus. This is my call as your mother, to lead you to God and show your love for Him by your service."* I could see Mary come dressed in blue and holding the Infant Jesus. Mary said: *"My dear children, I raise up my Son as an infant before you. You should understand, that when you look on each infant and think of the unborn, you should see my Son present in each of them. Remember His words, 'When you help the least in My Kingdom, you are helping Me.' Pray, my children, with a deep fervor to rid your country of this plague of abortion."*

Friday, September 20, 1996:

After Communion, I could see an empty pew and a bouquet of red flowers were placed on the seat. St. Therese came and said: *"My son, you are seeing empty pews to remind you of your mission to bring souls back to Jesus and back to His Church. You know how much I wish to help you in your missionary efforts. The priest mentioned how all of you are called to be apostles in witnessing to Jesus. This is a life long work, that you cannot rest on your past accomplishments. You must see each day as an opportunity to save souls. Keep fighting this battle against evil until your dying day."*

Later, I could see a horizontal plane, and it was directed toward Jesus who was on the cross. I then saw a bright light beam from a laser follow the plane, and it struck Jesus causing Him pain. Jesus said: *"My people, you are still testing Me today with the pain of your sin. For many, science has become worshipped as a god in your world. You have looked to science to answer all of your questions in life. When mysteries cannot be solved, you let science propose theories and you then treat these as fact. Many have come to believe in evolution, and a haphazard start of creation. These explanations have fallen, when the burden of proof cannot be found to substantiate them. You have taken adaptations to an environment to mean a total specie change. Yet, in all of your history, you have not seen one specie change its chromosomes to a higher number. You cannot expect order to come from disorder. All I have created is of its own origin, nothing has changed. You cannot see planets and the dust of space materialize from nothingness. Stars are born and die, but the matter and order of their nature conforms to My plan. Believe in My Creation as an act of My Will. Every time a man is born, I instill life in that being, and his plan of destination to be directed to Me. You have free will to believe whatever you please, but this does not change the nature of how I have created everything. See the errors in trusting only in yourselves and science. Come to me in love to show Me thanksgiving for all I have given you. Only I am worthy of praise and worship. Understand your place in life, and you will be happy to be one with Me."*

Saturday, September 21, 1996: (St. Matthew)

After Communion, I could see the heavens open and a magnificent display of God the Father coming. I then saw a serpent representing the devil and he opened his mouth. I could see a long deep tunnel down into the serpent. Jesus said: *"My son, I am showing you how Satan is leading many souls down the wrong path away from Me. Your messages bring a heavy responsibility on you. Be ever vigilant against the evil one in your life, and remember your prayers everyday. I am sending you out in My service as the apostles, to help lead the people back to Me. This is a time of opportunity for spiritual preparation, as no other event has occurred in history. Your mission is important and needs to be carried out in a most speedy manner. Take every opportunity I give you in spreading My Word. No matter how much you are harassed or are tired, you must go forward in my service when I call on you. Rejoice that you are called to go forth and preach My Word."*

Later, after Communion, (Steve & Paula's wedding) I could see a long line of people coming to a wedding feast. Jesus said: *"My people, I have told you that many will be called to My banquet, but few will be chosen. Some will come expecting to enter, but they will not be properly dressed in spiritual wedding garments, and will be turned away. To be properly ready, I have asked you many times to seek My forgiveness in confession before the priest. Do this while you still have time, or it will be too late to turn back. Once the evil one controls your life, it will take a great act of faith to be saved. Do not be concerned with what you will wear or what you will eat in this life. It is your preparation of your soul for the next life, or your spiritual life that matters most. I have asked you to be ever vigilant, and live your life as if you will die tomorrow, for you know not the hour of My coming."*

Sunday, September 22, 1996: (Children's Mass)

After Communion, I could see the entrance to a large brick Church. Jesus said: *"My people, I wish you could bring the children to Me in church, so they can be acquainted with My Word. By showing them example, the children will learn to visit Me at Church on Sunday and have respect for this day of the Lord. Over time the children will be understanding the words of the Gospel, if they meditate on the meaning or are taught the meaning. You parents have a heavy responsibility to teach My little ones the faith, but the best way to teach them, is by the way you live. When you live your faith, and show your children how you live what you believe, this will reinforce the lesson in My words. If the children see only what you say, and do not see it in your actions, then how do you expect them to follow My commands? Children are great imitators, and they will pick up all of your bad habits as well. Be watchful of your speech and your actions in front of the children, or you could give them the wrong message. If you teach My love, then show them My love in all of your actions, then you will truly be teaching them My Word in the best way possible."*

Later, I could see some spotlights on girls moving around in an awards show. I then could see a playing field with many baseball and football teams playing. Jesus said: *"My people, do not be taken up with your obsessions of awards in fame and glory. Such vainglory lasts but a moment, and it is quickly forgotten. Do not be seeking such things, since only the worldly like to show off, and have positions of authority. You must be humble and seek Me only, if you are to perfect yourselves. Again, do not waste your precious time with such frivolous pursuits, as constantly watching sports programs. Many have placed such sports even above Me as a god in their minds. If you are to be My disciples, I ask you to be a people of prayer, and not recreation for your own satisfaction. Your world is in most need of prayer to reconcile your many sins. Listen to My pleading in prayers for conversion, for peace and to end abortions. With so many reasons that your prayer is needed, how can you go on wasting your time on things that do not help your spiritual life? It is time now to get up, and moving to help Me, or you may be left waiting at My Gate to Heaven."*

Monday, September 23, 1996:

After Communion, I could see an altar in a brick Church and Jesus appeared to come through the wall with His arms outstretched. Jesus said: *"My people, I have looked on your world and many are taken up with themselves, instead of Me. If I cannot find enough people to give Me praise, I could raise up faithful from even the dead stones. My children, the evil one is very active in your world, and he is occupying your time with many distractions. He has so confused even My faithful, that many are seeking more after worldly affairs than giving time for Me in prayer and adoration. If you will not come to Me, then I will come to you in different ways, that will show you My ways are more important than your concerns. You busy yourself with tasks that have no relation to spreading My Kingdom. I am asking you dearly, My friends, to pay more attention to following My Will than your own. Do not let Satan distract you with so many worldly cares, that leave Me no time in your day. Place Me first in your day and do everything in My Name. Your tasks then will be a prayer, and you will make the time to honor and praise Me."*

Later, I could see a black limousine with a driver. Jesus said: *"My people, I wish to give you a lesson about pride. This sin is the most insidious, since many times it is the reason why many do not seek My forgiveness in confession. Pride causes a fear of embarrassment. It also causes a fear of the loss of your comforts. I call you sinners, which you are, but many do not want to admit it. This is why it is most difficult for some to seek Me in confession, since they are embarrassed to tell the priest their sins. Still others even fear being chastised by the priest. I tell you, My friends, come to Me and I will forgive you your sins, if you are sorry for them. I wish to give you My rest and restore your soul to the glory of a pure soul as it was before your sin. In order to be pleasing to Me, you must be humble and put aside your fears and love of the pleasures of this world. Shun fame and prestige among men. Instead, take My yoke of following My Will upon you, and you will experience My love and peace. When your soul finds its rest in Me, it will not desire things, but you will only want to love and be loved. This healing grace, I offer you in confession, is the beauty of My mercy. Continue to seek Me in these heavenly joys and your soul will reach its spiritual fulfillment."*

Tuesday, September 24, 1996:

After Communion, I could see a cross on a huge stone and I shivered physically as I sensed Jesus' Resurrection. Jesus said: *"My people, as you have seen my resurrection break the bonds of death and sin, so you are witnessing a new dawn of creation of My*

Church. I empowered My disciples after My death by the power of the Holy Spirit, to go out and spread My Good News of salvation. As you have seen the glory of this morning's dawn, know that My glory and grace shines upon all of My people. I have given man the power now to overcome his weaknesses in sin, but you must seek My graces through the sacraments to strengthen yourselves. Even now, My friends, I wish to announce to you that you again are about to see the dawn of a new age of My triumph and that of My mother. You should glory in eager anticipation, as you await the demise of all evil. Evil's reign will be brief, and then your hope in My victory will soon be realized. Have faith My people, and prepare for this one last battle. Once Satan is conquered, you will experience My love and peace to a pitch you cannot even fathom."

Later, I could see a rainstorm at night with a light shining on the road. Then, I could see a wind blowing the trees. Jesus said: *"My people, you are at the threshold of a changing world. If you continue to forget Me, and care more for your own concerns, you will see more trouble with the weather in gathering your crops, and more wars between the nations. Why do you not come to Me for help and seek My graces? I am willing to forgive you your sins and receive you into My arms. I pour My love out on you in the gifts I bring before you, but you do not thank Me, nor realize what you have, comes from Me. I tell you, My wrath of justice stands ready to condemn the wicked who ignore Me and commit all kinds of murders. For those who do good, they will be received into My bounty. Those who do evil, they will have their prized possessions ruined and stripped from them. You think My ways are unfair, but are not your ways against My commands? You do not have much time to convert and change your ways. See the imminence of My forthcoming justice, and choose to follow the narrow road to heaven. If you do not heed My wishes, then soon you will be brought to your knees by the weight of your sins."*

Wednesday, September 25, 1996:

After Communion, I could see a fish as a symbol and it was coming down out of the sky. Jesus said: *"My people, My apostles were fisherman, but fish have been mentioned frequently in the*

Gospels. When I told My apostles they would be fishers of men, this symbol of fish took on a whole new meaning for My early Christian family. Through the years, this fish symbol draws on the apostolic work of bringing men to conversion. It is by this symbol in this vision, that you understand all of My faithful are called on this mission. Some are called to be more active than others, but your baptism calls on each of you to spread the Gospel. Call on the gifts of the Holy Spirit to help you whenever you preach in My Name. It was the inspiration and grace of the Holy Spirit that strengthened My apostles to go forth from the upper room to teach all nations. So I ask all of My faithful, even now, to go forth and cast your nets, that you too may be fishers of men for God."

Thursday, September 26, 1996:

After Communion, I could see a triangle representing the Trinity with the stars of the heavens behind it. Then, I could see a pyramid and the darkness of evil in the occult. Jesus said: *"My people, the powers of holiness far surpass the power of the evil ones. Still, there are some seeking evil powers instead of their Creator. Why are so many concerned with the future that they seek fortune tellers, palm readers or tarot cards for their answers? Today, has troubles enough of its own. Do not be concerned with tomorrow, that you cannot change, and deal with the present which presses on you now. Fears and worries are useless. It is better to pray for My help to lead you through the day on faith. When you are doing your duty and following My Will, that will be enough for you to concern yourselves with. Do not be seeking other powers that could possibly invoke evil influences on you. Be content with your lot and be joyful each day to please Me by your good deeds and your prayers."*

Later, at the prayer group in Church, I could see spears or bishop hats surrounding the pope. Jesus said: *"My people, remember when I questioned those who came for Me in the garden. 'Am I a brigand that you must carry Me away?' Even so, My Pope son will be removed against his will. This will be a violation in the succession of popes, but evil will have its way for a time. See this schism in My Church is nearly upon you."* I could see some kind of a bank vault that held information on smart cards ready to be distributed to all the people. Jesus said: *"My people, be ready for when men will try to control your buying and selling. Great plans have been made by One World organizations to allow these smart cards to be put into circulation. Beware, My people, and avoid their plans, even if it be inconvenient for you to buy and sell. One day you will be forced to barter and go into hiding from such men."* I could see some spaceships launching satellites into orbit. Jesus said: *"My people, many of the satellites being placed into orbit will be used to locate and control people. Through the electronic devices that will link everyone to their banks, evil men will watch and control many. These satellites will be used for surveillance to follow people as well. This is why hiding in caves or at My refuges will protect you. Pray, My people, so you will follow My angels in your hour of need."* I could see Mary come and she was looking for those to pray and fight against the abortions. Mary said: *"My dear children, you make some attempts to fight abortions, but your people have hard hearts to change their views in supporting life. How long do you expect my Son to allow this carnage to continue? I have pleaded with you many times to fight and stop abortions. If they do not decrease dramatically soon, my Son's justice will fall upon you and I will not be able to hold back His hand."* I could see an open casket with a dead person laid out in it. Jesus said: *"My people, many times I have told you to be vigilant in prayer and fasting, so you are ready to face the judgment at any time. I have asked you, My son, to preach repentance for this in preparation for the tribulation. It is also proper to preach repentance at any time, since death may call on you when you least expect it. Prepare your life everyday as if it is your last. You cannot live in faith until you are ready to die in faith. Keep your soul clean with frequent confession, so you will be the wise servant waiting for your master's return."* I could see some children dressing for Halloween in their costumes. (An eclipse of the moon by the earth occurred this night.) Jesus said: *"My people, look for the signs in your skies for the omens to the coming events. Every large event has been preceded with such signs to give witness to the people. These signs will point to the evil one's coming much as when My star led those to Bethlehem. Wars will be given such signs in the sky. There have been such lights in the sky before some of your world wars. Read the signs of these times as history passes closer to the time of My victory. Live and have hope in My day, and I will grant you an era of peace beyond your imagination."* I could see a picture of Jesus as the Divine Love showering His graces and His mercy on us. Jesus said: *"My people, I thank you for being faithful to My Chaplet of Divine Mercy. I see many of you consecrating your lives to My service, and that of My mother. When you do so, I can act through you as instruments of My love. You become My hands, My voice and My feet to bring My Gospel to all nations. Strive to follow My Will and you will come closer to living in the Divine Will. Your soul will then find its joy in Me. Live in My One Body, so you can all live in the harmony of My plan for each of you."*

Friday, September 27, 1996:

After Communion, I could see an old wall as the Wailing Wall in Jerusalem. Jesus said: *"My son, I have given you messages before, that these signs in the sky will be times of unrest and wars. Do not be surprised when you see these things happening even in your papers now. The unrest you are seeing in My promised land is an example of when future eclipses will indicate the Battle of Armageddon as well. These signs are very obvious and a time when prayer for peace will be My calling in answer to these happenings. Man has been tested in many ways, but his differences over land ownership have caused many battles. See in all of these wars, it is man fomenting all of his own problems. Pray, My people, for a time is coming when all evil and wars will be done away with. This era of peace is not long off. Rejoice, that My victory will usher in a new age in your lifetime."*

Later, I saw a large grandfather clock in a hallway. Jesus said: *"My people, your time for conversion is running out. Now is the time to repent as John the Baptist heralded Me in the dessert. Before the tribulation starts, you must prepare yourself spiritually, so you will be able to withstand the demons with My help. This is the time you should grow closer to Me in hope and faith. I give you hope in the purification of My victory over evil. This, also, is the time I must send My laborers out for the harvest of souls. So many of My people have been misled, that they need direction and purpose in coming back into the fold of My sheep. It is never too late to convert from your sins, but it will be much harder in the face of this evil. Without grasping My hand in the light I shine through the darkness, most will not find their way back to Me. Prepare now with your holy weapons of My Sacraments and the Rosary. Have joy and trust in My Word, that I will deliver you through My protection as I did My people in the Exodus. Encourage others to forgiveness in confession, and you can help strengthen others in this battle as well."*

Saturday, September 28, 1996:
After Communion, I could see an old book as a Bible in a Church setting. Jesus said: *"My people, I am happy to see My faithful are striving to preserve the traditions of My Church. You have seen many changes in the Mass. Still, I ask you to receive My gifts of the Mass and the sacraments as a legacy of My love that you must hold dear to your hearts. Do not be concerned with change, for My laws and My gifts are changeless. I am the Creator and you are My creatures, created to love, serve and adore Me. Lead the people to Me in adoration before My Blessed Sacrament. See My Real Presence I leave with you, so you can remain a part of My Body at all times. Treasure the sacredness of My Presence by prayer and your faithfulness to My service. Never lose sight of following My Will in what you do each day. Your daily prayers are a testimony for your everlasting love for Me. Keep close to Me through confession, prayer and your acts of mercy. Strive, My people, to be one with Me in perfection, so you can live with Me in the Divine Will. The more you preach My Word before men, the more I will strengthen you in your apostolic work."*

Later, I could see a large metallic object on a train in the shape of a long cigar. It was revealed to me that this was a large magnet for making Tesla weather machines. Jesus said: *"My people, I have warned you that some of your food problems may be contrived. You may have thought that food supplies may be controlled to create shortages. In your vision you are seeing an even more devious means of controlling food could be done by controlling your weather. These machines can influence your weather through various wave patterns put out by huge electromagnets.*

You have men in various places who are planning to use these devices in destabilizing your weather patterns. Evil has reached new levels of controlling people by their electrical devices. Pray, My people, for My deliverance from such evil men. Even despite all of their devious plans, I will use ways to thwart them from reaching their goal of world control. I will baffle their devices, so many will not even work. You will see My hand come upon them and help you avoid them. Pray continually, that My faithful will keep faith and trust in Me for your protection. I will watch over your souls by empowering My angels to work in your behalf to frustrate the evil men's plans. My power will be shown you and you will wonder why men will even challenge Me at all."

Sunday, September 29, 1996:

After Communion, I could see a ring of lights. There was someone dragging a cloak around Our Lady that pictured her Assumption as if to cover it up. Mary came and said: *"My dear children, many people do not want to recognize how my Son has blessed me. You understand how some people do not want to give me honor as the mother of Jesus, and mother of all men, as Jesus directed through St. John the apostle. Even though I may receive criticism, I love all of these people just as Jesus does. Continue to encourage my Scapular and Rosary as weapons against the evil one. I am watching over all of you as a faithful mother. You have asked about working on Sunday, even when it is a hard choice. I ask you if you would give a gift to my Son by your reverence in not working on Sunday. It is part of keeping the Lord's Day holy that you should honor this request. It is even a Church law not to do any servile work on Sunday, but many have disregarded this law, thinking their needs are more important than honoring God. Give this day especially over to my Son, and make it a day of prayer and doing His work alone."*

Monday, September 30, 1996:

After Communion, I could see some footprints in stone. Jesus said: *"My people, as you hear the story of Job, you can understand how it is for someone to be tested. Even though you complain about your lot, you do not appreciate how others suffer unless you walk*

И. ТЕРЕЛЯ

Архангел Михайло

in their footsteps. Try to help your neighbor in his need, for there are always those worse off than you are. While some are looking at how many are better off than they are, they should be grateful for the gifts I have given them. Take a lesson from Job when difficulties come your way. Worse things could happen, and these little tests should strengthen your faith. Do not be so concerned with gaining and keeping possessions of the world's wealth, but strive more to be rich in heavenly things of the next life."

Later, I could see a bright sunny day with shops selling food along the road. Then I saw large pieces of bread like matzo being carried down the middle of the road by children. Jesus said: *"My people, I wish to assure you that I will feed you with My Heavenly Bread as in the communion St. Michael delivered to the children in several apparitions. You will have My Presence given to you to strengthen your faith during the tribulation. Many of My angels will be called upon to give you this Daily Bread. It truly will be called the Bread of Angels. Do not fear, My people, what you are to eat or if you will receive enough to fill your stomachs. Some of the Saints have lived on My Eucharist alone, since I am the fulfillment of your soul. I will test your faith with this purification, but you will see that this is indeed a proper preparation for you, to live in My Divine Will in the following era of peace. Yes, you will suffer for a while, but your suffering will bring on My victory that all mankind is awaiting. Share this message with all, since what I will be feeding you, will be both for the soul and the body."*

Index

Prepare for the Great Tribulation and the Era of Peace

confession
  admit you are sinners (Jesus)   8/30/96
  changing world (Jesus)   9/24/96
  pray for poor souls here (Jesus)   8/27/96
  save souls (St. Therese)   8/14/96
  stiff necked people (Jesus)   8/30/96
  time is short (Jesus)   8/13/96

conversion needed
  stiff-necked people (Jesus)   8/2/96

creation
  beauty of body and soul (Jesus)   7/26/96
  vs. evolution (Jesus)   9/20/96

cross
  freedom from sins (Jesus)   9/19/96
  life's decisions (Jesus)   9/6/96
  purify self by suffering (Jesus)   9/10/96

crosses
  Divine Will in peace & love (Jesus) 8/5/96
  follow these few years (Jesus)   8/23/96

dead stones
  can praise Him (Jesus)   9/23/96

death culture
  TWA 800 flight (Jesus)   8/26/96

detention centers
  AntiChrist (Jesus)   8/11/96
  persecution/relig/political (Jesus) 8/21/96
  tortured & martyred (Jesus)   9/12/96
  New World Order police (Jesus)   7/17/96

disasters
  more frequent (Jesus)   9/4/96

diseases
  in tribulation (Jesus)   9/19/96

Divine Will
  follow in everything (Jesus)   9/23/96

droughts & floods
  chastisements (Jesus)   8/30/96

earthquakes
  increase & intensity (Jesus)   8/31/96

eclipse
  signs & omens of war (Jesus)   9/26/96

elections
  decision for USA (Jesus)   9/19/96
  money vs moral decay (Jesus)   8/19/96

electrical devices
  communications (Jesus)   8/21/96

electronic connections
  Antichrist's hypnotism (Jesus)   7/17/96

end times
  battle of good and evil (Jesus)   7/20/96

Era of Peace
  effect on animals (Jesus)   9/16/96
  in lifetime (Jesus)   9/27/96
  live in the Divine Will (Jesus)   9/30/96

evangelize
  beauty of saving souls (Jesus)   9/10/96
  before/during tribulation (Jesus) 7/31/96
  especially in family (Holy Spirit) 8/11/96
  pray with people (Jesus)   9/9/96
  save souls (St. Therese)   9/20/96

evangelizing
  messages for purifying (Jesus)   7/28/96

events increasing
  fears of the end times (Jesus)   7/19/96

evolution
  vs. creation (Jesus)   9/20/96

Fall events
  watchful of your souls (Jesus)   7/17/96

false prophets
  discernment of fruits (Jesus)   8/5/96

famine
  futures market (Jesus)   9/1/96
  plan for food shortages (Jesus)   8/1/96

prepare people & nations (Jesus)   8/26/96
store one year's food (Jesus)   8/7/96
tribulation (Jesus)   8/30/96

famine world wide
  tell everyone/governments (Jesus) 8/19/96

fire purification
  choose Me or the world (Jesus)   7/14/96

fishers of men
  gifts of the Holy Spirit (Jesus) 9/25/96

flooding
  animal sanctuaries lost (Jesus)   7/24/96

food
  contrived shortages (Jesus)   8/7/96

food and shelter
  Jesus will provide (Jesus)   7/17/96

food damage
  bad weather & insects (Jesus)   7/24/96

forgiveness
  in Confession (Jesus)   9/14/96

Fr. Luke Zimmer
  petition for healing (K. Tekakwitha) 7/28/96

Garcia grotto
  pulsating crucifix (Jesus)   7/20/96

generosity
  more given/more expected (Jesus) 8/4/96

Gospel
  daily walk with Jesus (Jesus)   8/7/96

Government leaders
  bankers (Jesus)   8/28/96
  hide from these killers (Jesus)   7/17/96

healings
  must heal souls first (Jesus)   7/31/96

hearts
  open to mercy & love (Jesus)   7/24/96

heaven on earth
  angels & safe havens (Jesus)   9/13/96

hiding
  detention/mark of beast (Jesus)   7/31/96
  some martyred/protected (Jesus)   7/25/96

Holy Communion
  bridge to spiritual life (Jesus) 9/2/96

Holy Spirit
  Betania reunion (Holy Spirit)   8/11/96
  upholds remnant Church (Jesus)   9/18/96

humility
  please God only (Jesus)   9/1/96

hurricane Fran
  chastisement (Jesus)   9/4/96

Job
  test of faith (Jesus)   9/30/96

judgment
  convert today (Jesus)   8/9/96
  repent and prepare (Jesus)   9/26/96
  use of talents (Jesus)   9/2/96

justice
  God's vs man's judgments (Jesus) 9/5/96

killing
  Lord of life and death (Jesus)   8/27/96

liberation theology
  priests (Jesus)   9/3/96

light in the darkness
  devil talking in your ears (Jesus) 7/13/96

love
  follow His Will (Jesus)   9/18/96
  harmony with God's Will (Jesus)   7/21/96

love of Jesus
  Do you love Me? (Jesus)   8/3/96

mark of the beast
  buying food (Jesus)   9/4/96
  chip gives Satan control (Jesus) 8/20/96

marriage
  lessons for success (Jesus)   8/11/96

Prepare for the Great Tribulation and the Era of Peace

Mass
preserve traditions (Jesus) 9/28/96

medals of Marian shrines
evangelize and convert (Jesus) 7/15/96

media
controlled,press present (Jesus) 7/31/96

mercy
forgive 70 x 7 times (Jesus) 9/15/96

messages
concern over dates (Jesus) 9/12/96
conferences & books (Jesus) 9/5/96
Mary waning,Jesus incr (Mary) 7/30/96
personal evangelization (Jesus) 9/9/96
personal mission (Jesus) 8/30/96
personal mission (Mark) 8/16/96
personal responsibilities (Jesus) 8/17/96
personal/books/speaking (Jesus) 7/26/96
seek conversion of souls (Jesus) 8/6/96
speak truth (Jesus) 9/3/96
warning and preparation (Mary) 7/24/96

messengers
face serious opposition (Jesus) 8/2/96
will suffer hardships (Jesus) 7/16/96

messengers & prophets
prepare the people (Jesus) 8/29/96

mission
spread His Word (Jesus) 9/21/96

money
cannot serve 2 masters (Jesus) 8/3/96

moon
blood red, sign (Jesus) 9/19/96

Mother Cabrini
visit shrine (Mother Cabrini) 9/19/96

Mother Cabrini Shrine
visit healing waters
(Mother Cabrini) 8/14/96

nuns
role of women (Jesus) 8/14/96

object of all love
soul's thirst for the Divine (Jesus) 8/21/96

occult
do not seek other powers (Jesus) 9/26/96
evil spirits/false witness (Jesus) 7/31/96

Olympics
focal point of love (Jesus) 7/24/96
smart card,terrorism (Jesus) 8/14/96
technology mark beast (Jesus) 7/17/96

peace
prayers for pride (Jesus) 8/28/96

perfection
fast, pray, give money (Jesus) 9/12/96
sin as impediment (Jesus) 9/15/96

permanent signs
trust in protection (Jesus) 8/25/96

persecution
apostasy in Church (Jesus) 9/13/96

plane crash
a witness in prayer (Jesus) 7/24/96

poor people
money & suffering (Jesus) 8/25/96

Pope John Paul II
last pope (Jesus) 9/17/96
schism, exiled from Rome (Jesus) 8/16/96

prayer
do not waste time (Jesus) 9/22/96
Our Lady's intentions (Mary) 9/7/96

prayer groups
help hiding/unify people (Jesus) 7/27/96

prepare
with sacraments & rosary (Jesus) 9/27/96

pride
body's mortality/testing (Jesus) 8/20/96
fear of embarrassment (Jesus) 9/23/96

Prepare for the Great Tribulation and the Era of Peace

suffering
  struggles of life (Jesus) — 7/29/96

Sunday
  pray and do not work (Mary) — 9/29/96

talents
  fulfill God's plan (Jesus) — 8/31/96

terrorism
  rivalry of Jews & Arabs (Jesus) — 7/27/96

terrorism increasing
  innocent lives in abortion (Jesus) — 7/19/96

Tesla
  standing wave patterns (Jesus) — 9/28/96

testing time of life
  handling misfortunes (Jesus) — 7/15/96

Transfiguration
  Moses/Elijah messages (Jesus) — 8/4/96

trials
  persevere in love (Jesus) — 9/18/96

tribulation
  diseases,famine,manna (Jesus) — 8/17/96

triumph
  demise of all evil (Jesus) — 9/24/96

United Nations
  one world government (Jesus) — 8/11/96

United States
  separation church & state (Jesus) — 8/7/96

volcanoes
  cause 3 days darkness (Jesus) — 7/23/96

vultures in Israel
  Battle of Armageddon (Jesus) — 7/18/96

war
  bankers & oil interests (Jesus) — 9/4/96
  commemorate Hiroshima (Jesus) — 8/6/96
  escalation in Iraq (Jesus) — 9/4/96

warning
  repent (Jesus) — 8/29/96
  time of enlightenment (Jesus) — 8/21/96

wars and rumors of wars
  love your enemies (Jesus) — 7/14/96

weapons
  spiritual & physical (Jesus) — 8/24/96

weather in fire and water
  chastisements for sin (Jesus) — 7/13/96

weather machines
  contrived food shortages (Jesus) — 9/28/96

wedding banquet
  many called, few chosen (Jesus) — 9/21/96

wise virgins
  prepare food (Jesus) — 8/30/96

worldly desires
  keep proper priorities (Jesus) — 9/18/96

More Messages from God through John Leary

If you would like to take advantage of more precious words from Jesus and Mary and apply them to your lives, read the first three volumes of messages and visions given to us through John s special gift. Each book contains a full year of daily messages and visions. As Jesus and Mary said in this volume:

> *Hear my messages and read again the old messages that you may realize these words of warning and preparation are for your age at this time.* Mary 6/24/96

> *...there will come a time when you will be banned from speaking and you will rely on your books to spread the message.* Jesus 6/26/96

> *Listen to my words of warning, and you will be ready to share in the beauty of the second coming.* Jesus 7/4/96

> *I will work miracles of conversion on those who read these books with an open mind.* Jesus 9/5/96

> *Learn to appreciate all the messages, even the older ones, so you may complete your perfection in knowing My Will.* Jesus 9/12/96

Prepare for the Great Tribulation and the Era of Peace
Volume I - *Messages received from July 1993 to June 1994*
    ISBN# 1-882972-69-4 . . . . 256pp. - $7.95

Volume II - *Messages received from July 1994 to June 1995*
    ISBN# 1-882972-72-4 . . . . 352pp. - $8.95

Volume III - *Messages received from July 1995 to July 11, 1996*
    ISBN# 1-882972-77-5 . . . . 384pp. - $8.95

Visit your local bookstore for other great titles from:

QUEENSHIP PUBLISHING

Call of the Ages - *Thomas W. Petrisko*
The Apparitions and Revelations of the Virgin Mary
Fortell the Coming Fall of Evil and an Era of Peace
ISBN# 1-882972-59-7 . . . . $11.95

Trial, Tribulation and Triumph - *Desmond A. Birch*
Before, During and After Antichrist
ISBN #1-882972-73-2 . . . . $19.50

Mary: God s Supreme Masterpiece - *Fr. Bartholomew Gottemoller*
ISBN# 1-882972-48-1 . . . . $5.95

Jesus, Peter and the Keys - *Scott Butler, Norman Dahlgren, David Hess*
A Scriptural Handbook on the Papacy
ISBN# 1-882972-54-6 . . . . $14.95

The Gift of the Church - *by Monsignor Bob Guste*
Current Questions and Objections about the Catholic Church and
Down-to-Earth Answers
ISBN# 1-882972-01-5 . . . . $7.95

The Coming Chastisement - Br. Craig Driscoll
ISBN #1-882972-41-X $1.95

The Light of Love - Patricia Devlin
My Angel Shall Go Before Me
ISBN #1-882972-53-8 . . . . $8.75

Marian Apparitions Today - Fr. Edward D. O'Connor
Why So Many?
ISBN #1-882972-71-6 . . . . $7.95

The Truth about Mary, Volume I - Robert Payesko
From Human Inventions to the Truths Taught by Scripture
ISBN # 1-882972-82-1 . . . . $8.95

The Truth about Mary, Volume II - Robert Payesko
Mary in Scripture and the Historic Christian Faith
ISBN #1-882972-83-X $9.95

The Truth about Mary, Volume III - Robert Payesko
A Response to Fundamentalist Misconceptions and a Return to
Historic Christianity
ISBN #1-882972-84-5 . . . . $10.95